modern terrarium studio

Design + Build Custom Landscapes with Succulents, Air Plants + More

Megan George of The ZEN Succulent
Photography by Michelle Smith

Fons&Porter
CINCINNATI, OH

contents

For my beloved Nana — a woman worth remembering.

introduction

I grew up in a home filled with greenery. One of my earliest childhood memories is of the large glass terrarium that sat proudly in the corner of the foyer at my Nana's home in southern North Carolina. It was a floor model, standing over five feet tall (1.5m), full of lush houseplants that quietly crept up its enclosure walls over the years. The terrarium, made by my mother and father in the mid 1980s shortly before they married, is shaped similarly to a groovy 1970s lava lamp. I was drawn to that terrarium, always pressing my nose and hands against the glass, curious to explore the beautiful landscape inside—something I do even now, more than twenty years later.

When I opened my modern terrarium and craft business, The ZEN Succulent, the first piece I created was a succulent terrarium; I gravitated to the unique textures, shapes and colors of these particular plants. This was the beginning of my succulent obsession, an obsession that now includes tillandsia air plants and living landscapes.

Terrariums have become popular in recent years, but their history dates back as early as the nineteenth century. After having trouble maintaining healthy ferns outdoors in the polluted London air, Dr. Nathaniel Ward noticed that a tiny fern and grass seed had sprouted in the damp soil contained in a covered jar that also held a cocoon he had been studying. As he continued to observe this unintended occurrence, he noticed that evaporated moisture from the soil condensed on the glass during the day and ran down and back into the soil in the evening, creating a humid, self-contained environment. Dr. Ward published works on his discovery of these miniature greenhouses, later called the Wardian cases, which were early versions of the modern terrarium.

Modern Terrarium Studio was written with the goal of learning more about the world of succulents and air plants through projects that explore different terrarium designs. The first part of the book focuses on what you need to start your succulent and air plant terrariums, gives basic instructions on how to maintain your plants' health and discusses key elements of terrarium design that will make yours unique. The second part provides step-by-step instructions for creating your own terrariums perfect for everyday decorating and presents clever ways to incorporate living landscapes into your special occasion décor.

While writing this book, I spent countless hours creating and expanding my succulent and air plant knowledge. Taking time to just create and perfect my craft was beautiful and calming. I hope that the living landscapes in this book help you find peace as well. With each project, your confidence will grow, you'll develop your own preferences and techniques, and eventually you will master each design, elevating them with your own personality and aesthetic.

Happy making,
Cheers!

getting started

THIS CHAPTER IS FILLED with my personal advice for terrarium creation, gleaned from years of working successfully with succulents and air plants. We'll go over the basic foundation for each terrarium, how to choose the right plants for any landscape, which containers are best and how to use simple accents to great effect.

The information in this chapter will become a point of reference when questions arise about plant care and design. As you create and care for your own terrariums and landscapes, you too will develop your own tips and pointers based on your own experiences with each plant, have fun learning from it.

tools + materials

The tools listed here are useful when creating or caring for the terrariums and living landscapes mentioned in this book. A few specific tools may be needed for individual projects; those tools are discussed within the projects themselves.

TOOL	USE
E6000 glue (1)	Plant-safe glue used to attach air plants and other materials to a variety of surfaces; choose clear glue for an invisible finish
Embroidery floss (2)	Hang, attach and tie plant materials safely together; also can be used as a colored accent.
Floral wire (3)	Secure air plants to wood or other plants.
Gardening gloves	Protect hands during planting.
Hammer (4)	Hang terrariums and add decorative nails.
Mini tubing cutter (5)	Cut brass rods for himelli planters
Newspaper	Protects work surfaces and can be used to handle cacti.
Paintbrushes (6)	Brush dirt off plants and for other general cleanup.
Pencil	Good to mark material placement when designing living landscapes.
Pruning shears	Cut back succulent roots, remove damaged or withered leaves, and collect cuttings from overgrown plants; cut wood for arrangements.
Scissors (7)	Cut floss and shape preserved reindeer moss and moss materials; can use to trim plants as well.
Spray bottle (8)	Mist the plants as needed between watering; can be used to water air plants.
Tweezers	Place pebbles, seashells, wood or any other accent materials into the tight spaces that a wooden dowel might not reach.
Watering can	Cans with long, narrow spouts work best for precise watering of container arrangements.
Wire cutters	Cut floral wire.
Wooden dowel (9)	Position plants for planting as well as any other small materials during terrarium creation.

2
1
E6000
9
6
3
5
8
4
7

basic layering materials

SUCCULENT AND PLANT TERRARIUMS

When making a succulent and plant terrarium, the basic layering materials provide the foundation for the entire living landscape. Without these simple ingredients, the terrarium will not have what it needs to grow and flourish for years to come.

These are the layers, in order of how they should be assembled:
First layer: sand and/or stones
Second layer: activated charcoal
Third layer: cactus and succulent soil mix
Fourth layer: plants and decorative elements

SAND AND/OR STONE LAYER FOR DRAINAGE

All terrariums, whether they contain succulents, tillandsia air plants, cacti, moss or other plants, lack drainage holes (they are not like planters). Because of this, terrariums must have some way to remove water so the plants' root systems won't be damaged. Sand and/or stones such as gravel are the perfect natural way to do just that. Sand and stones come in a variety of colors and finishes, from natural, matte tones to colored, polished neons; explore your options. Before using any sand or stones they need to be cleaned with water and dried to rid them of any harmful residue that might negatively impact the plants. Throughout the book, sand or stones (sometimes both) are used to help with drainage in succulent, cacti and moss terrariums.

ACTIVATED CHARCOAL LAYER FOR FRESH SCENT

Through terrariums, you bring the outdoors into your own indoor space, but it's important to leave the damp, murky woodland smells outside. To keep your terrarium smelling fresh, a thin layer of activated charcoal will do the trick.

CACTUS AND SUCCULENT SOIL MIX FOR DRAINAGE AND NUTRIENTS

Succulents and cacti thrive when the soil they are in drains easily and does not retain too much water. A specialized soil blend such as a cactus and succulent mix and cactus, palm and citrus potting mix are perfect premixed options. These mixes provide the needed drainage plus a boost of nutrients that encourages root growth and bloom development. Traditional potting soil can be used as well, but avoid gardening soil; it retains too much moisture.

EMBEDDING PLANTS AND ADDING DECORATIVE ELEMENTS TO COMPLETE YOUR DESIGN

The final layer for all living terrarium landscapes is the carefully planted plants. To provide additional color and complete your design, additional decorative materials can be used, which we discuss later in this section.

AIR PLANT TERRARIUMS

Air plant terrariums have slightly different needs and therefore require different layers. Only two layers are needed:

First layer: filler base materials

Second layer: plants and decorative elements

FILLERS (ANY DRY SURFACES OR MATERIALS)

When making a tillandsia air plant terrarium, there's only one rule for the first layer: Anything goes, as long as it is naturally dry. Unlike succulents and other plants, air plants do not need soil to grow and thrive. In fact, they must be placed on a dry material (called a filler); if placed on a wet or damp material (such as soil), the constant moisture will cause the plant to rot and eventually die. Examples of dry surfaces and materials we use in this book include natural sand, colored stones and pebbles, dried distressed wood, and preserved reindeer moss and moss materials.

PLACING PLANTS AND ADDING DECORATIVE ELEMENTS TO COMPLETE YOUR DESIGN

After your base materials are in place, simply add your air plants. Air plants can be grouped with a variety of plants in the succulent and bromeliad families and many other plant types; this is how they grow in their natural habitat.

Air plants can also be mounted or placed on branches, plants or wooden pieces using floral wire, embroidery floss or E6000 glue to secure them. We'll explore these techniques in various projects later in the book. To provide additional color and texture, add decorative elements to complete the design.

container selection

When thinking of terrariums, the first image that might come to mind is one of lush plants encased in glass vases. After all, glass provides a great platform to see the beautiful landscape from all angles, including the layers below the surface. However, terrariums can be elevated to new heights of creativity when you try other containers as well. From cappuccino cups to syrup containers, vintage lanterns to laboratory beakers, almost any container—as long as it's watertight and without drainage holes, no matter the size—can be used to create one-of-a-kind living landscapes. You can even venture beyond glass and containers altogether by using items from branches to bicycle rims to contain your creations.

When choosing a vase or container, listen to your personal style and aesthetic and visualize the setting and location where you would like to place your terrarium. This can help narrow down your vessel options. Here a few basic (and important) questions that can also help you decide which container is right for you:

Is the container drainage hole-free and watertight? Unlike many planters, terrariums do not have drainage holes.

Will the plants be visible once inside the vessel? Clear glass vessels are always a great option for terrariums because you can easily see the plants and other elements inside; slightly tinted colored vases can work beautifully as well.

Will plants fit comfortably and flourish? Almost all succulents grow well together, but many grow at different rates and even in different directions; this is true for air plants as well. Sometimes this is hard to predict. Ask questions when purchasing plants and be prepared to learn through trial and error as your plants begin to grow in their vessel. Make any changes as needed.

Does the container complement the plants inside? The vessel can further enhance the living landscape in many ways: by bringing out certain hues and textures found in the plants, by enhancing the shape of certain plants or by adding a much-needed element of simplicity.

If you answer "yes" to these questions as you consider a container, you are well on your way to finding the perfect vessel and creating your terrarium.

A majority of the terrariums mentioned in this book are open terrariums, meaning that they do not have lids to fully enclose the plants inside. Succulents and air plants thrive in terrariums that are open because they provide great air circulation, which is essential for the plants to remain healthy and continue to flourish. Avoid placing succulents and air plants in completely closed containers if you want them to last.

Closed terrariums, terrariums completely enclosed with lids, are great options for mosses, tropical houseplants and ferns, just to name a few. The closed container creates the humid environment that those plants need to thrive.

decorative elements + accents

Terrariums are naturally full of color and texture. Adding decorative elements and accents can enhance the natural beauty of your chosen plants or take the design in an unexpected direction. For example, adding natural-colored sand and a handful of pebbles can transform your cactus terrarium into a desert oasis. Adding a few seashells and a sea fan to a terrarium with an air plant usually found in the rainforest changes the mood of the terrarium from tropical to beachy.

A variety of decorative elements such as Spanish moss, preserved and colored reindeer moss and distressed wood are explored in this book, but the possibilities are endless. Accent pieces such as larger stones, clay mushrooms and even miniature figures can change the mood and feel of a terrarium, as you'll see in several projects. Don't be afraid to experiment with a wide variety of materials and colors. You're limited only by your own creativity.

unconventional features

You might notice ordinary and not-so-ordinary objects that could work inside your terrarium or even as the surface of the landscape itself. Some of my best ideas begin when something unique catches my eye. Walking through flea markets, I might see a rusted bicycle and think, "That would look great polished up and suspended in the air with terrariums hanging from it," or while driving downtown, crumbling concrete might inspire me.

Here are some unconventional terrarium and living landscape features (some you might find looking around the house) that might further spark your creativity, some of which we will explore in this book:

- concrete
- restored bicycle rim
- dried seed pods
- leather
- wooden slabs
- brass pipes
- lighting fixtures
- grapevine branches
- toys and figurines
- preserved sea fans
- game pieces (Monopoly pieces, Scrabble letters)
- vintage keys
- embroidery floss
- ceramic tiles
- crystals (amethyst, quartz, etc.)

plant selection

Succulents and air plants both come in a vast variety of sizes, textures, shapes and colors. With so many options, you might feel overwhelmed when selecting your plants. Here are a few things to keep in mind:

SIZE

When selecting plants for your terrarium, always first consider the size of the plant in relation to your design. A 6" (15cm) potted aloe will fit inside an 8" (20cm) vase, but will not leave room for other succulents and possible accents. Switching to a smaller 3" (8cm) potted aloe provides space for more plants as well as other accents, giving you a more complete terrarium design. Throughout this book, we focus on terrariums that use potted plants measuring between 2" (5cm) to 6" (15cm), but will primarily focus on arrangements that require 3" (8cm) to 4" (10cm) pots.

COLOR

From deep greens and pale blues to vibrant pinks and creamy pastels, the color palette of succulents and air plants cannot be rivaled. When creating arrangements, use the color of the plants as inspiration, grouping similar hues such as the pale greens of a burro's tail *(Sedum morganianum)* alongside the haunting whites of a ghost plant *(Crassula graptopetalum)*. The resulting arrangement is calming and peaceful. Add a single dark, glossy Zwartkop *(Aeonium arboreum)* with deep burgundy leaves to the same arrangement for something more passionate.

TEXTURES

Spiky, smooth, fuzzy and everything in between: Like color, the individual textures of each plant play a role in the feel of the arrangement. Explore textures and use them to make a statement.

LIGHT

Whether sunlight or flourescent light, all plants need light to thrive. When creating your terrarium, select plants based their on lighting needs. All terrariums, no matter what plants are used, should avoid direct light at all costs. The glass container used to house many terrarium designs will act as an oven when placed in direct light, killing the plants inside. Despite this similarity, different terrarium plants have different lighting needs that should be considered before grouping plants together.

Bright-light plant options The majority of succulents and all tillandsia air plants thrive in bright, indirect light, including aloes, panda plants *(Kalanchoe tomentosa)*, flapjack plants *(Kalanchoe luciae)*, zebra plants *(Haworthia fasciata)*, Perle von Nürnberg *(Echeveria)*, jade plants *(Crassula ovata)* and all tillandsias.

Low-light plant options Some succulent varieties have adapted to low-light environments and can live in a terrarium placed in low light. Such succulent plants include many haworthias and aloe vera. Most mosses also thrive in low light.

top 25 plants to use in your terrariums

This list of succulents and tillandsia air plants are my go-to plants for a variety of living landscapes. I've turned to them time and time again. Each of these plants brings something unique to a design.

The plants on this list can be purchased locally at your neighborhood garden center in the warmer months of the year or shipped directly to your doorstep from growers all over the United States. You'll work with the plants on this list throughout the book, along with many others. Like the majority of plants used in the projects, these plants are easy to care for within any terrarium or living landscape.

1

2

3

4

5

1. **Zebra plant *(Haworthia fasciata)*** is one of my favorite terrarium plants. This small evergreen succulent plant has pointed leafs that are adorned with white stripes (just like a zebra), making it a great feature plant.
2. ***Tillandsia caput-medusae*** is an air plant with twisting leaves, a velvety texture and rich red blooms in spring and summer months. This air plant can grow close to 10" (25cm) tall and provides fullness to any living landscape. Tuck it into distressed wood for an eerie yet polished effect.
3. **Panda plant *(Kalanchoe tomentosa)*** is a succulent with thousands of microscopic white hairs on a single leaf and distinctive brown patched tips. It is a widely grown terrarium staple; also look for it in a beautiful golden brown color.
4. ***Tillandsia streptophylla*** is an air plant native to Central America, Mexico and the West Indies. Its silvery green leaves twist underneath it. Watch for a bright red sprout in blooming season.
5. ***Tillandsia capitata* 'Peach,'** with its boldly colored peach and pink tips and purple blossoms, provides a punch of color during the bloom season wherever placed.

6

7

8

9

10

6. **Blue chalk sticks *(Senecio serpens)*** is a fleshy succulent with slender, pale blue-green leaves often seen outdoors, but also perfect for indoors. Use this as a go-to succulent when your design needs additional height and color contrast.
7. **Hens and chicks *(Sempervivum)*** come in many different color variations and shapes, from hardy olive to bright lime, touches of purple to red, all with various leaf textures and sizes. The largest plant is called the hen; it's surrounded by smaller plants (the chicks). Use them together in your arrangement or separately.
8. ***Echeveria* 'Perle von Nürnberg' hybrid** is a beautiful rosette-shaped succulent with symmetrical pale gray leaves that gently turn to pink at the center. This soft-colored plant is perfect for breaking up an abundantly green design.
9. ***Tillandsia* 'Eric Knobloch' hybrid** is a tall, large hybrid of a *Tillandsia brachycaulos* and *Tillandsia streptophylla*. It is considered a king among other species with its vibrant green, spiraling leaves; its crowning achievement comes in blooming season when its leaves boast a frosty rose hue. It makes a perfect statement plant.
10. **Flapjack plant *(Kalanchoe luciae)*** leaves are uniquely shaped like matted green pancakes; they bunch together and tumble down the shaft of the plant. Some varieties have vivid red edges.

11

12

13

14

15

11. **Jade plant *(Crassula ovata)*** has many shiny, rich green leaves reaching upward from a thick trunk. Some varieties of jades can reach 5' (1.5m) tall indoors, but for terrariums, stick to smaller varieties such as 'Gollum', 'Hobbit' and 'Mini Jade.' They can fill out any landscape, no matter the theme.
12. ***Tillandsia ionantha*** is an air plant that can pop into tight spaces. It is found in a range of colors from dark green ('Guatemalan') to blushing red ('Fuego'), some even a fading yellow ('Druid'). The size is generally 1"–2" (2.5cm–5cm), or 4"–5" (10cm–13cm) for larger varieties.
13. ***Tillandsia hondurensis*** has soft, silvery leaves that look as if they are in motion, with its roots reaching out. Watch them blush with hints of pink during their blooming season.
14. ***Haworthia reinwardtii*** rises from the soil in olive green and burgundy columns. The succulent is a great low-level filler for arrangements.
15. **Lavender scallops *(Kalanchoe fedtschenkoi)*** have large bluish green leaves that are breathtaking, with scalloped edges in cream and pink that look as if they've been handpainted. This succulent grows erect, perfect for adding color to the ground level of your terrarium.

16

17

18

19

20

16. ***Faucaria stomatium*** is a bold, low-level succulent that seems to grow nestled one atop the other. It has hardy green leaves outlined by white stripes and dots and touches of pink.
17. ***Tillandsia xerographica*** is a stunning beauty with silver leaves that cascade downward. It commands attention even in the simplest of containers.
18. **Fairy washboard *(Haworthia limifolia)*** has spiraling evergreen rosettes. Unlike other haworthias, the fairy washboard has flat yet very robust evergreen leaves; because of this, they'll need a little more space in your living landscape.
19. **Mountain aloe *(Aloe marlothii)*** is not your typical aloe; it has a spiny, textured surface and horn-shaped leaves. It works well in rough desert landscapes or more dramatic pieces.
20. ***Echeveria* 'Lola'** is a rosette succulent with a natural ombré effect, gently fading from pale green to a light shade of violet, ending in a pale pink. Its elegant shape makes it popular in bridal bouquets.

21. ***Tillandsia stricta*** is one of the most common air plants. Though its stem is bright pink, it blooms purple. There are many different hybrids of all sizes, each with straight, fanned-out leaves.
22. ***Tillandsia brachycaulos abdita*** has glossy red leaves that fan out in all directions. I love to place it among different shades of green preserved mosses for great color contrast.
23. ***Tillandsia magnusiana*** is a wispy ball of threadlike leaves; it requires careful consideration before placing it into a terrarium due to its fullness. It is a personal favorite.
24. **Aloe 'Walmsley's Bronze'** is one of the easiest succulents to grow; it also quickly provides many offsets (other smaller plants), which can be separated and replanted easily. Its pointed, fleshy green leaves turn a brilliant bronze and it works well in any terrarium.
25. ***Anacampseros rufescens*** has olive leaves that build to a rich, jewel-tone purple; increase the light it receives for an even more intense color. With its clustered, star-shaped leaves, this small rosette succulent can easily blend into a landscape of soft, petal-like succulents or hard, horned succulents.

plant add-ons

Other varieties of plants can be added to your terrariums to provide a little extra texture, color, height or coverage. These miniature plants should be purchased in 4" (10cm) or smaller pots. Don't overuse these plants; they can easily overpower the arrangement.

When added thoughtfully, these plants can further enhance the arrangement and better highlight the featured plants. Here are some great plant add-ons for terrariums and other living arrangements, some of which we use throughout this book.

MOSSES AND FERNS

Selaginella mosses, cushion moss *(Leucobryum)*, rock cap moss (*Dicranum*), haircap moss *(Polytrichum commune)*, fern moss *(Hypnum)*, clump moss, natural tropical moss, sheet moss, Elzevir fern *(Nephrolepis exaltata)*, house ferns

CARNIVOROUS PLANTS

Venus flytrap plants *(Dionaea muscipula)*, sundew plants *(Drosera)*, low-growing American pitcher plants *(Sarracenia)*, warm-temperate butterworts *(Pinguicula)*

TROPICAL PLANTS

Hoya 'Hindu Rope' plants, nerve plants *(Fittonia verschaffeltii)*, African violets (saintpaulias), *Peperomia caperata* 'Variegata'

All of the plants listed can also be used as a main feature in terrarium designs. Please note that these add-ons might require additional care, pruning, feeding (carnivorous plants only), fertilizing and watering.

plant care

In addition to choosing succulents and air plants with great texture, color and height, you also need to choose plants that are healthy. Before placing any plant in your terrarium, inspect all the leaves and remove any that are discolored, damaged or withered. Most plants will have spent some time outdoors; always check carefully for insects on the plant. Remove any insects before purchasing or simply choose a new plant.

SUCCULENTS

Succulents are found most often in dry deserts and semi-deserts all over the world. There are over fifty different plant families that can be classified as succulents, all of which come in a wide range of unusual shapes, textures, patterns and colors. Succulents are characterized by their thick leaves and stems, which is where they store water during dry conditions; they are drought tolerant, therefore easy to maintain. Their basic care instructions are listed below.

Light. A majority of succulents require bright, indirect light, especially when inside a glass container. Placing by a window, in a room with natural lighting or with fluorescent light is required to maintain its health indoors. If your plants develop tall and thin stems and/or the leaves are fragile and discolored, it is a sign of too little light; increase the light slowly.

Water. The key to keeping succulents happy is to water them weekly (sometimes waiting even longer, up to ten days during the winter months) and sparingly. Gently pour water directly into the terrarium around the edges of the plants. Do not pour water directly on the leaves, as it could harm the plant. Do not overwater; let the soil dry out between waterings. An easy way to judge watering amounts is based on the container size.

OVERWATERING AND UNDERWATERING SUCCULENTS

Signs of overwatering: discolored (yellow or white) leaves, soft leaves, the plant is not growing. If caught early, remove all dead leaves and take the plant out of the arrangement to check the roots. If the roots are brown (healthy roots are white) and rotted, remove them immediately and replant it into the container. Reduce the amount of water given to the plant and monitor its health to see if it recovers. If it does not, remove it permanently from the terrarium. Other signs of overwatering include plants that have rotted completely, as if melted onto the soil. In this case, the entire succulent should be removed and replaced with another healthier plant.

Signs of underwatering: brown spots on leaves, leaves drop off. If caught early, remove dead leaves and increase the amount of water or water more frequently. Remember, succulents need more water during the spring and summer months.

BASIC WATERING AMOUNTS BY CONTAINER SIZE	
Small container (5"–7" [13cm–18cm])	Water ¼ cup (2 fl oz) weekly
Medium container (8"–10" [20cm–25cm])	Water ½ cup (4 fl oz) weekly
Large container (11"–14" [28cm–36cm])	Water 1 cup (8 fl oz) weekly

The summer months are a period of growth for many succulents; because of this, they may need more water. During the winter months, succulents may require less frequent watering, every 10–14 days or as needed. Use your best judgment when watering based on the soil; keep the soil moist to the touch but not wet. Only water a succulent when the soil is dry; this will help prevent rotting.

Air circulation. Make sure that the succulents are in a container and location that is well ventilated.

Growth cycle and blooming. Succulents actively grow during the spring and summer seasons, eventually going dormant in the autumn and winter. During the dormant period, succulents prefer temperatures between 45–55°F (7–13°C), which helps the plant form flower buds. All succulents bloom; the colors, patterns and length of the bloom vary from plant to plant.

Fertilizer. To further enhance the succulents' health, a low-balanced, soluble fertilizer such as 10-10-10 formula can be used as instructed, but is not required.

AIR PLANTS

Air plants, also known as tillandsia, are native to warmer climates and can be found in deserts, tropical rainforests and mountain regions. By adapting to so many environments, air plants vary greatly in texture, color and size. It is widely believed that air plants only need air to survive (it's in the name after all) and do not need any water at all: This is simply not true. Air plants require watering, air circulation and light but are easy to maintain, requiring minimal care; their basic care instructions are listed below.

Light. All air plants require bright, indirect light, especially when inside a glass container. To keep your air plants healthy, place them by a window, near a fluorescent light or outdoors in a shaded area.

Water. When watering, remember to water the entire plant, not just the roots (if the air plant has them). There are three popular and effective ways to water your air plants: misting, submerging or rinsing. All plants will need to be watered more frequently in drier climates or warmer weather and less frequently during colder weather.

Misting is suggested throughout this book for watering air plant arrangements. When misting, use a spray bottle to heavily mist the entire surface of the plant two to four times a week or as needed. When your air plant is inside a terrarium, take the plant out to mist or simply mist inside the container. If misting inside a container, mist only the living plant. Do not mist as heavily but just as frequently.

For plants that are mounted to elements of the terrarium or design (such as a wreath), misting allows you to water the plant without removing the plant from the design.

To water the plant by **submerging**, soak the plant in cool water once a week or as needed for twenty to thirty-five minutes. Submerging is a good option for larger tillandsia air plants to make sure that every part of the plant gets enough water. Submerging can also work for plants that are mounted.

To **rinse**, place the air plant in your hand and gently run cool water over it using a sink or shower head for about two to three minutes, two times a week. Rinsing requires removing plants from their normal display but it is good to thoroughly water air plants, especially plants secured on wood or rocks.

To prevent water from being trapped between the plant's leaves (which will cause the leaves to rot), flip the air plant upside down after watering and gently shake off the excess water. Let it dry out before placing it back into the container (this is not necessary if you're misting the plant).

Air circulation. Air plants love fresh air. Make sure your air plant is in a container and location that is well ventilated.

Growth cycle and blooming. Air plants grow throughout the year (depending on their environment) and produce offshoots called "pups" when mature. These offshoots are the beginnings of a new plant. Air plants also produce seeds that are released when the plant blooms. Time of year when the bloom occurs, bloom duration, flowering color and size of bloom vary from species to species.

Fertilizer. To further enhance the air plant's health, a high-nitrogen fertilizer such as 10-5-5 plant food can be used about once a month, but is not necessary. Use fertilizer as instructed.

OVERWATERING AND UNDERWATERING AIR PLANTS

Signs of overwatering: Air plants only take in as much water as they need, so overwatering is rarely an issue. However, if air plants do not dry out between watering, their leaves can rot, which cannot be repaired. To prevent this, remember to always let the plant dry after watering and place the plant on a dry surface with good air circulation.

Signs of underwatering: curled, shrivelled and brown dead leaves. If caught early, remove all dead leaves from the plant and submerge the plant in water for five hours or overnight, letting it dry afterward. Monitor its health to see if it recovers its color and the leaves return to normal.

PLANT HEALTH

Cleanliness is important for everything, and living landscapes are no different. You must keep your containers clean in order to keep your succulents, air plants and other greenery healthy. Regularly remove all moisture and dust from glass containers. When you see discolored, damaged or withered leaves and/or faded blossoms, remove them immediately; this helps prevent fungus.

The leading killer for living succulent and air plant landscapes is mold, caused by overwatering and poor air circulation. If your landscape shows signs of mold, immediately remove the molded area, replace the soil and trim the leaves and stems as needed. If you notice mold in over 40 percent of the terrarium, completely discard the contents of the terrarium (including plants and wood accents; stones and other washable pieces might be salvaged and cleaned with hot water—use your best judgment). Wash the container with hot water and start over.

Like mold, insects and pests can be a side effect of overwatering. A succulent or air plant terrarium with too much moisture becomes an ideal humid habitat for insects looking to lay their eggs in the soil. If you see insects around or inside your landscape, immediately remove the infected area. Depending on the severity of the infestation, this might require uprooting the plant and removing the soil. Use insecticide as needed and instructed.

planting succulents, cacti + air plants

Before planting, clean out the terrarium vase or container with hot water; this will remove any potentially harmful residue that might damage your plants. Next, prepare the plants. Any plants that require soil (including succulents) should be "barefoot." This means the soil in the plants' roots should be gently removed. If your plant has extremely long roots (over 4" [10cm]), carefully clip the ends of the roots back 1"–2" (2.5cm–5cm) using pruning shears or scissors; this doesn't harm the plant and will make planting easier.

Once the succulents are barefoot, prepare the terrarium soil: Add water to the soil until it feels damp to the touch. To plant, dig a hole large enough for the plant's roots and place the plant inside, making sure all roots are covered and firmly in the soil.

Some of the terrarium designs in this book call for the use of cacti, which are a type of succulent. They are planted in essentially the same way as other succulents, except that care should be taken when handling cacti with spines. Use either gardening gloves or a sheet of newspaper folded horizontally several times to protect your hands.

Air plants are not planted in soil. Instead, place them or mount them on a naturally dry surface; sand, gravel and preserved reindeer moss all work well for this. You might notice when placing your air plants that some plants have strawlike pieces coming out of the bottom; these are their roots. Not every air plant has roots and some varieties develop roots over time. Unlike succulents, these roots are not made to collect nutrients and absorb water but to help them hold on to trees, branches and other surfaces in nature. Air plant roots can easily be hidden in your terrarium or living landscape by carefully burying them into the terrarium filler layer or gently tucking them to the side. It is not recommended to remove roots from air plants; they are closely attached to the base of the plant and removing them may damage the plant's structure.

Once you finish planting your succulents or placing your air plants, there may be a little soil or sand on the plants' leaves from planting; gently dust it off with a paintbrush. Brushing off the dirt gives your arrangement a more polished, modern look, but also helps keep the plants healthy.

terrarium + living landscape design

Texture, color and plant size all play an important role in the design of each terrarium or living landscape. The designs in this book follow my own personal design style; natural with a contemporary edge, I strive to create modern landscapes that look like they were pulled straight out of their respective environments. To do this, I group bold plants together and place them throughout the arrangement. I encourage you to experiment with your own terrarium and landscape designs, creating designs that reflect your own personal aesthetic. Below are a few key pointers to help you get started with your own designs.

Set a theme. Choosing a theme gives your terrarium a unified design. You may come up with a theme first and choose your plants and accents accordingly, or you may find yourself drawn to certain plants that inspire a theme of their own; either process works. Many of the projects in this book are based on a theme, so you'll see firsthand how a theme comes together.

Choose the main attraction. It all starts with one plant, your feature plant. This is the plant that you really want to showcase for any reason, be it texture, color or size, and that your arrangement is inspired by (but not necessary centered around). Build your terrarium or living landscape around the feature plant with supporting greenery (plants with similar or complementary textures, colors or shapes).

Create levels. In all terrarium and living landscapes, the best way to display the plants is to design with different height levels in mind: bottom level, mid level and top level. These slight differences in height create fullness and add interest to the arrangement. You can also utilize decorative elements and accents to add dimension to the arrangement.

Test out arrangements. When figuring out the placement and layout of your design, utilize your empty container: You can position the plants inside first without planting to give yourself a better feel for how the plants work in the specific space. Laying the plants out on newspaper can also allow you to see how certain plants work together before you actually begin planting.

choosing the setting + styling

Creating your terrarium or landscape is only one part of terrarium design. You also need to choose a location to display the terrarium. I like to display terrariums in places where family and friends frequently gather. A large, leafy green succulent arrangement on a cherry wood coffee table helps set the mood for warm conversations. You may find that gazing at a living wood arrangement resting on the corner of your desk brings you inspiration and relaxation. Try hanging an air plant terrarium in front of a bright kitchen window or trade the lamp on your bedside table for an arrangement of single potted mosses in simple containers at varying heights.

Terrariums can add a unique touch when decorating for special events as well. Display a variety of different-shaped apothecary vases filled with carnivorous plants to add color and character to an evening dinner party. Once the festivities are over, the vases can be separated and placed in various locations throughout the house for everyday enjoyment.

Once you find the perfect location for your terrarium, try grouping it with other items, such as books, figurines, pottery or other potted plants for an even more stylish display. Throughout the book, you will see examples of how to style the projects presented. Use the photographs as inspiration for your own designs.

Remember that both succulents and tillandsia air plants need bright, indirect lighting to flourish indoors. Good locations include near windows facing south, east or west and in rooms with fluorescent light. In the summer months (or in areas with a warmer climate year-round), terrariums or living landscapes featuring succulents and air plants can be placed outdoors (briefly) for special occasions as long as they are in shaded areas.

terrarium + living landscape projects

IN THE FOLLOWING PAGES are projects to put your new plant knowledge to use while making something modern, fresh and beautiful in the process. When thinking up these projects, I wanted each to be special, with its own theme or look for everyday enjoyment. At the same time, I wanted projects that would excite and challenge beginners while also inspiring seasoned crafters to take each exercise further and make it their own. I hope you'll use these exercises and pictures as a starting point and let your own creativity shine.

My favorite containers to use for terrariums are those made of glass. I love how each terrarium layer is clearly defined and how the plants can be effortlessly viewed from all angles. You'll see many projects that utilize glass containers, while exploring how to craft living landscapes out of natural and even unconventional materials.

I often receive questions from people asking how to add greenery to their events and special occasions in unexpected ways outside of the normal flower centerpieces. As an avid dinner party guest and occasional host, I wanted to share some of my favorite living landscape designs that can add a "wow" factor to any special event with tips on how to include them. These special event designs can be found toward the back of the book. Now, it's time get our hands a little dirty.

a vibrant shore

HANGING AIR PLANT TERRARIUM FEATURING SEASIDE ELEMENTS

air plants

Tillandsia ionantha 'Mexican'

Tillandsia ionantha 'Rubra'

Tillandsia capitata 'Peach'

materials

7" (18cm) glass ball hanging vase

Preserved reindeer moss in 3 colors

Sand

Preserved sea fan pieces in red/orange color

3 Haitian candy-striped tree snail shells

2 white nipple shells

1. **Add the sand and preserved reindeer moss.** Gently fill the container with sand until just below the opening. Take a handful of each color of reindeer moss and arrange it inside, placing the darkest color toward the back and the lightest color in front. Bury the ends of the moss in the sand.
2. **Add the sea fans and place the air plants.** Tuck the sea fans into the arrangement, one resting in the back near the darkest moss and the other closer to the front. Next, arrange and place the air plants as desired, tucking them into the sand or resting them atop the moss.
3. **Place the shells.** Place a few shells throughout the terrarium. Group them around the plants or scatter them loosely in the sand. Hang the completed terrarium in bright, indirect light. Mist the plants twice a week or as needed.

living wreaths

GRAPEVINE WREATHS FEATURING BILLY BUTTONS

air plants

10–12 of the following plants per wreath:

Tillandsia butzii, Tillandsia capitata 'Peach,' *Tillandsia flabellata* 'Rubra,' *Tillandsiaa harrisii, Tillandsia ionantha, Tillandsia scaposa, Tillandsia streptophylla, Tillandsia stricta,* Spanish moss (*Tillandsia usneoide*)

materials + tools

Three 6" (15cm) grapevine wreaths

Preserved reindeer moss

Preserved moss-covered branches

6 preserved Billy Buttons *(Craspedia)*

E6000 glue (optional)

Several floral pins

1. **Arrange the air plants and preserved reindeer moss.** Place 10–12 air plants and the preserved reindeer moss on top of each wreath. Do not attach your air plants until you are happy with the placement. In the example, I've grouped the air plants on half of each wreath, leaving the other half of the wreath exposed.
2. **Tuck in air plants and preserved reindeer moss.** Once the layout is finalized, lift up the grapevine branches and gently tuck the air plants and reindeer moss into place. To better secure the plants, use E6000 glue as needed (optional). Be aware that if you use the glue, you won't be able to adjust your plants if you're not happy with the layout.
3. **Add additional pieces to complete.** Trim the stems of the billy buttons to 2½" (6cm). Tuck them into the grapevine branches along with the small, preserved moss-covered branches and floral pins; this creates a full and textured look. In my arrangement, I placed billy buttons on 2 of the wreaths and floral pins on the third. Hang the trio together or separately in bright, indirect light; mist the air plants twice a week or as needed, leaving the air plants on the wreath.

cascading rock collection

TABLETOP SUCCULENT TERRARIUM FEATURING TURQUOISE STONES

succulents

3" (8cm) potted *Anacampseros*

Two 3" (8cm) potted *Crassula ovata* 'Hobbit'

3" (8cm) potted *Haworthia attenuata radula* 'Hankey Dwarf Aloe'

3" (8cm) potted *Portulacaria afra* 'Elephant Bush'

4" (10cm) potted *Graptosedum* 'Vera Higgins'

Two 3" (8cm) *Crassula graptopetalum* 'Ghost Plant'

4" (10cm) potted *Pachyveria*

3" (8cm) potted *Euphorbia spiralis* 'Spiral Spurge'

3" (8cm) potted *Haworthia chloracantha*

materials

10" × 4" (25cm × 10cm) glass cylinder pan vase

Sand

Cactus and succulent soil mix

Activated charcoal

Decorative turquoise stones

Large turquoise mineral rocks (Utah Lake rocks used in example)

1. **Add the sand and turquoise stones.** Gently fill the bottom of the vase one-fifth full with a layer of sand. Add a layer of turquoise stones filling the vase another one-fifth full.
2. **Add the charcoal and soil, then arrange the mineral rocks.** Place a thin layer of activated charcoal over the stones then add the soil mix, filling the vase another one-fifth full. Arrange the turquoise mineral rocks close together in the center of the vase, leaving a 2" (5cm) gap between them. Use some remaining soil to build a small hill around the gap; this provides the base for the succulents to cascade downward.
3. **Arrange the plants.** Unpot all the plants and remove any soil from the roots. Arrange the plants, creating the illusion of them gently growing on top of the soil and cascading down the hill. Carefully plant each succulent starting from the center of the vase.
4. **Add more turquoise stones.** Use the turquoise stones to cover any visible soil. Place the terrarium in bright indirect light. Water the plants once a week, or more frequently as needed.

naturally wrapped

AIR PLANT TERRARIUM FEATURING MANILA ROPE

air plants

Tillandsia streptophylla

Tillandsia stricta soft leaf

Tillandsia ionantha 'Guatemalan'

materials

6" × 6¼" (15cm × 16cm) clear glass vase

Crushed coral sand

Preserved reindeer moss

Preserved lichen

Rattan bunch branch*

14" (36cm) manila rope, ⅝" (16mm) thick

*A great substitute for rattan bunches are walnut shells; they provide the same look but may be easier to find.

1. **Add the sand.** Pour the crushed coral sand evenly into the glass container, filling it one-fifth full.
2. **Create height with the manila rope.** Twist the manila rope into an S-shape and place it flat in the container. Lift the center of the rope to create more height and dimension.

3. **Add the reindeer moss and preserved lichen.** Place bits of preserved reindeer moss throughout the container at different heights. Fill in any gaps with pieces of preserved lichen.
4. **Add the rattan bunch branch.** Add a single rattan bunch branch to the arrangement. If you can, work it into the twist in the rope for a more unique look.
5. **Add air plants.** Place the air plants in the terrarium, arranging them at different heights. Keep the terrarium in bright, indirect light. Water air plants twice a week or as needed. Take the air plants out of the terrarium to water them; misting them in the container may cause the preserved lichen to mold.

colored air plant orb

AIR PLANT TERRARIUM FEATURING DOUBLE-OPENING VASE

air plants

Tillandsia ionantha 'Rubra'

Tillandsia ionantha 'Guatemalan'

materials

6" × 5½" (15cm × 14cm) open glass orb

Colored sand

Two 2"–3" (5cm–7cm) pieces of colored slate*

Preserved reindeer moss

Wooden twig (small enough to fit inside orb)

Preserved Billy Button *(Craspedia)*

*Slate rocks are available at floral supply stores.

1. **Pour the sand.** Fill the bottom of the container evenly with sand, stopping before the sand reaches the openings.
2. **Add the preserved reindeer moss.** Divide a handful of preserved reindeer moss into two separate bunches; place them in the container.
3. **Place the slate.** Position one piece vertically and the other horizontally within the container. These pieces of slate add dimension to the terrarium.
4. **Add the supporting items.** Place the twig and preserved billy button inside the terrarium, pushing the billy button firmly into the sand.
5. **Place the air plants.** In the example shown, I've placed one air plant near each opening. Set your finished terrarium somewhere with bright, indirect light. Mist plants twice a week or as needed.

plant world

AIR PLANT + SUCCULENT TERRARIUM FEATURING DISTRESSED WOOD

air plants

Tillandsia funkiana

Tillandsia capitata 'Peach'

Spanish moss (*Tillandsia usneoides*)

succulents

5" (13cm) potted *Kalanchoe luciae* 'Flapjacks'

3" (8cm) potted *Kalanchoe fedtschenkoi* 'Lavender Scallops'

3" (8cm) potted *Crassula ovata* 'Hobbit'

4" (10cm) potted *Crassula ovata* 'Hummel's Sunset'

4" (10cm) potted *Haworthia fasciata* 'Zebra Plant'

3" (8cm) potted S*enecio serpens* 'Blue Chalk Sticks'

3" (8cm) potted *Adromischus maculatus* 'Calico Hearts'

3" (8cm) potted *Anacampseros*

Various sedums

materials + tools

12" (30.5cm) glass globe

Cactus and succulent soil mix

Activated charcoal

Decorative gravel

10" (25cm) ghost wood piece or any unique piece of wood

Paintbrush (optional)

E6000 glue or floral wire (optional)

1. **Spread the stones and gravel.** Gently place decorative stones evenly into the glass globe, filling it one-fifth of the way. Where there are gaps in between the stone, spread one cup of decorative gravel (these smaller stones add more dimension to the terrarium and will provide additional drainage when fully assembled).
2. **Lay the charcoal and soil mix.** Place a thin layer of activated charcoal followed by the soil mix filling the globe another one-fifth full. Make sure to keep your container clean; if needed, use a paintbrush to dust off any soil that might stick to the glass.
3. **Arrange and plant the succulents.** Unpot the succulents, removing any soil from the roots. Arrange the succulents; I suggest grouping the larger plants in the center and moving outward with the smaller plants. Be sure to leave room for the decorative wood piece.

Once you're happy with the arrangement, plant the succulents, starting with the larger middle plants and working your way out.

4. **Add supporting materials.** Place the decorative stones around the outer plants and add the decorative wood piece.

5. **Add the air plants and display.** Complete the design by resting the air plants on the wood piece (use E6000 glue or floral wire to secure the air plants if needed). Place the finished terrarium in bright, indirect light. Water the succulents once a week and the air plants twice a week (by misting or rinsing if attached to the wood), or as needed.

jug band forest stompers

SUCCULENT + MOSS TERRARIUM FEATURING MINIATURE FIGURINES

succulents

3" (8cm) potted *Crassula tetragona* 'Miniature Pine Tree'

3" (8cm) potted *Crassula ovata* 'Hobbit'

3" (8cm) potted *Haworthia attenuata radula* 'Hankey Dwarf Aloe'

Two 3" (8cm) potted *Portulacaria afra* 'Elephant Bush'

Two 3" (8cm) *Adenium obesum* 'Desert Rose'

3" (8cm) potted *Aloe* 'Pepe'

3" (8cm) potted *Senecio articulatus* 'Candle Plant'

mosses

Various sedum mosses

Haircap moss *(Polytrichum commune)*

tropical plants

5" (13m) potted *Hoya* 'Hindu Rope'

materials + tools

8" × 2½" (20cm × 6cm) porcelain serving bowl

3½" × 2½" (9cm × 6cm) cappuccino cup

'Jug band' figures, N scale* (or any set of miniatures)

Cactus and succulent soil mix

Activated charcoal

Stones

Sand

Decorative rocks

2 miniature timber culverts, HO scale*

E6000 glue

*Both the jug band figures and the timber culverts I used are from Woodland Scenics, a brand that specializes in model railroads. N scale and HO scale refer to the size of the figures.

1. **Build the culverts and add the terrarium layers.** Assemble the set of culverts following the manufacturer's instructions. Set them aside to dry (depending on which culverts you purchased, you may also need to paint them). Add the layers to the serving bowl: Place a layer of sand in the bottom, filling it one-fifth of the way. Next, add the stones, again filling the bowl one-fifth of the way followed by a thin layer of charcoal. Finally, fill the rest of the bowl with cactus and succulent soil mix. Repeat the process to fill the cappuccino cup: Begin by placing the cup at an angle, resting it on its handle. Having the cup at an angle makes it easier to display the contents.
2. **Lay out the plants and bury the culverts.** Place the two containers side by side, leaning the cup against the bowl at an angle. Place the culverts across from each other, one in each container, at the point where the containers touch; the goal is to create the illusion that the culverts lead from one container to the next, creating a path for your miniature band. Plant the culverts firmly into the soil, then add soil on top and around them, so they are visible but partially underground.
3. **Add the plants.** Unpot all the plants and remove any soil from the roots. Carefully plant the large succulents first, then surround them with the smaller plants. Fill in with moss as needed to complete the plant landscape.

4. **Add supporting materials.** Use sand to create a thin path for your band to follow through the terrarium: Start at each culvert and wind the path through each terrarium. To create more dimension, add a few decorative pebbles and rocks to act as boulders within the terrarium landscape.
5. **Mount the miniatures and display.** Arrange the jug band miniatures and place them firmly into the ground. You can also place the miniatures on top of rocks: Place a tiny dab of E6000 glue on the bottom of the miniature and firmly press it onto the flattest surface. Place the terrariums in bright, indirect light, keeping the terrariums side by side. Even though these terrariums are housed in separate containers, they create a single cohesive landscape. Water once a week or as needed.

wooden geometry

AIR PLANT WALL DECOR FEATURING GEOMETRIC STRING ART

air plants

Tillandsia filifolia

Tillandsia capitata 'Peach'

Tillandsia ionantha 'Guatemalan'

Tillandsia stricta stiff leaf

materials + tools

Wood oil

Wooden board*

10" (25cm) suede cord

Pencil

Hammer

9 steel box nails (size 4D × 1½" [4cm])

Embroidery floss in 4 colors

Paper towel or cloth (for applying wood oil)

*Any flat piece of wood or wooden board can be used to create the base for your hanging air plant display. For this landscape, a solid olive oak wooden cutting board had the perfect natural design and came with a predrilled hole, perfect for hanging.

1. **Oil the wood and hang the cord.** Lightly cover your board with oil and gently rub it into the surface of the wood using a paper towel. This will prevent the wood from splitting. Because my board is olive oak, I used olive oil for this step. Tie the ends of your suede cord together, then pull the loop through the hole in your board, threading one end of the loop through the other. If possible, hang your wood from the loop against a wall (use your finger instead of a nail); this allows you to find the natural center of the piece.
2. **Mark and hammer the nails.** With your pencil, lightly mark where each nail will go on the front of your board. You may want to sketch a few designs before marking the board. Keep the nails somewhat evenly spaced, filling up the board as much as possible. Hammer each nail in place, leaving 1" (2.5cm) of the nail exposed.
3. **Wrap the embroidery floss.** Start with one color of floss and tie the end tightly to a nail. Pull the floss to an adjacent nail, and wrap the floss around the nail several times. Pull the floss to another nail, again wrapping it several times. Repeat this process as many times as you would like, creating triangles. When you finish one color, wrap the floss around the same nails in the same order, creating a second layer of floss. Tie the end of the floss around the last nail to secure. Use the other colors to fill in the rest of the design, making sure all colors have a double layer of twine.

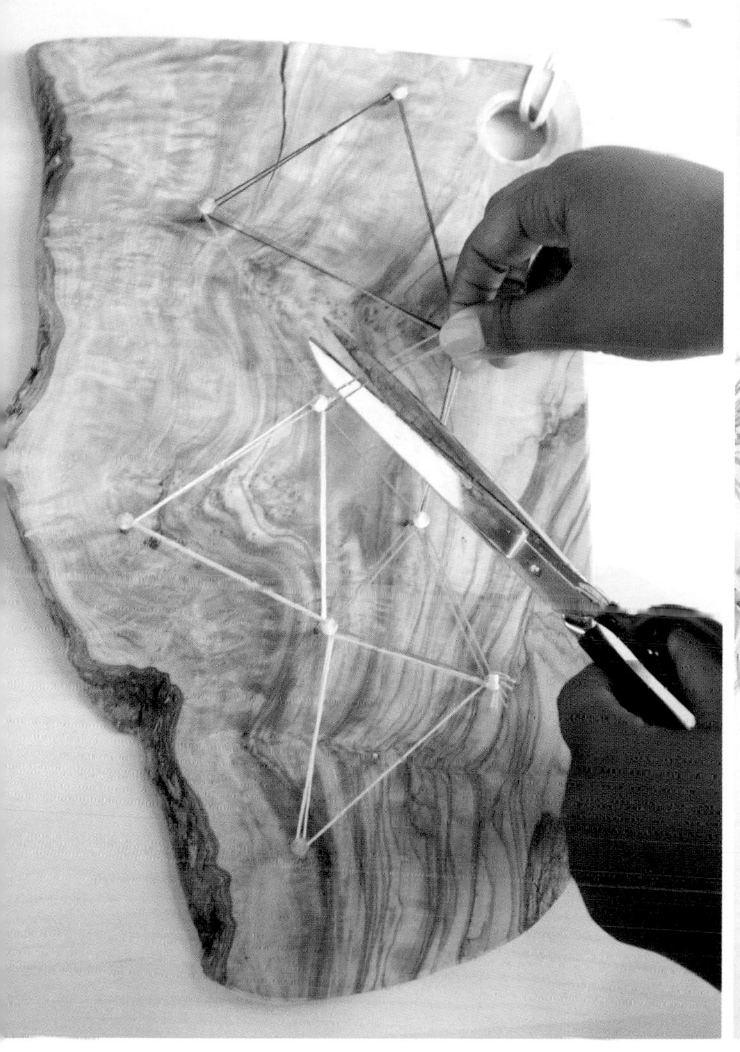

4. **Trim the embroidery floss.** Once all ends have been knotted and secured, trim away the excess floss, taking care not to cut your design.
5. **Add the air plants and hang.** Tuck the air plants between the two layers of floss and hang the completed board in a location with bright, indirect light. Mist the plants twice a week or as needed.

rooted in moss

MOSS & SUCCULENT TERRARIUM FEATURING DECORATIVE WOOD ROOT

mosses

Fern moss *(Hypnum)*

Clump moss

succulents

Several *Sempervivum cebenese* 'Hens and Chicks'

materials + tools

5½" × 3¾" (14cm × 9.5cm) glass bowl

Ornamental potting stones

Activated charcoal

Potting soil*

Tree root (or distressed wood)**

Pruning shears

*Potting soil works best for growing moss.

** I found this root in my backyard and cut it to fit the container, but a unique wooden stick can create the same effect.

NOTE

The tall, leafy plant pictured in the terrarium is a paper mulberry plant. It sprouted up unexpectedly after the moss terrarium was complete. I kept it in the arrangement because of its unique leaf shape, but had to remove it after a few weeks to keep it from crowding the container.

1. **Lay the stones and charcoal.** Pour the potting stones evenly in the bottom of the bowl, filling it one-fifth full. The stones act as the foundation for the moss; this will help with drainage. Place a thin layer of activated charcoal on top of the stones.
2. **Create a slope with the soil.** Pour the soil into the bowl, again filling one-fifth of the bowl. Build one side up higher than the other, creating a small hill inside the terrarium.
3. **Cut and place the root.** Use pruning shears to cut the root or branch to fit in the bowl. Place the root on top of the soil, following the slope of the hill you created.
4. **Plant the moss and succulents.** Plant the moss around the root, filling in both sides of the bowl. Use the sharp end of the pruning shears to poke holes in the moss. Plant the succulents directly into the moss, pushing the roots through the holes in the moss and directly into the soil.
5. **Add the stones and display.** Scatter a few decorative stones throughout the terrarium to complete the natural look. Place the terrarium in indirect light. Water the moss generously once a week or as needed. Take care not to overwater the succulents.

structural brass planters

HIMMELI HANGING PLANTER FEATURING BRASS TUBING

air plants

Tillandsia aeranthos × stricta

materials + tools

36" (91cm) of ⅛" (3mm) brass tubing (for small himelli)

30 yards (27m) of 30-gauge non-tarnish brass wire

Mini tubing cutter

Scissors

Ruler

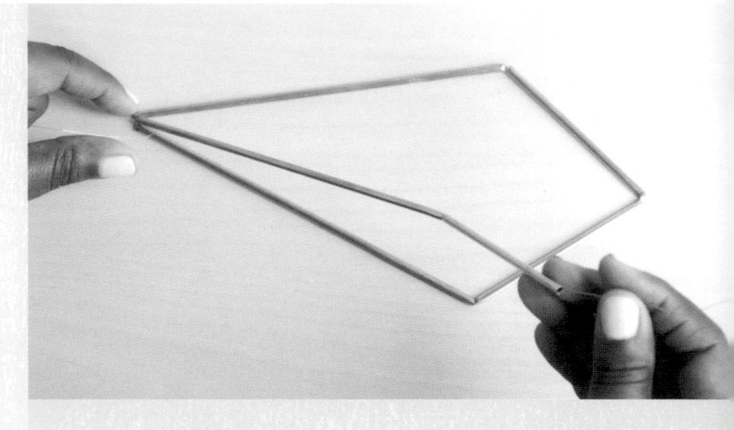

NOTE

The directions are for the small himelli only. To make the larger himelli, follow the directions to make the small himelli, then make a larger himelli using six 6" (15cm) and three 12" (51cm) pieces of brass tubing (you'll need 108" [274cm] total). Use the same method as the small himelli to make the large himelli. Place the smaller planter inside the larger and top with a wooden bead. Complete the look with *Tillandsia stricta* 'Stiff Purple.'

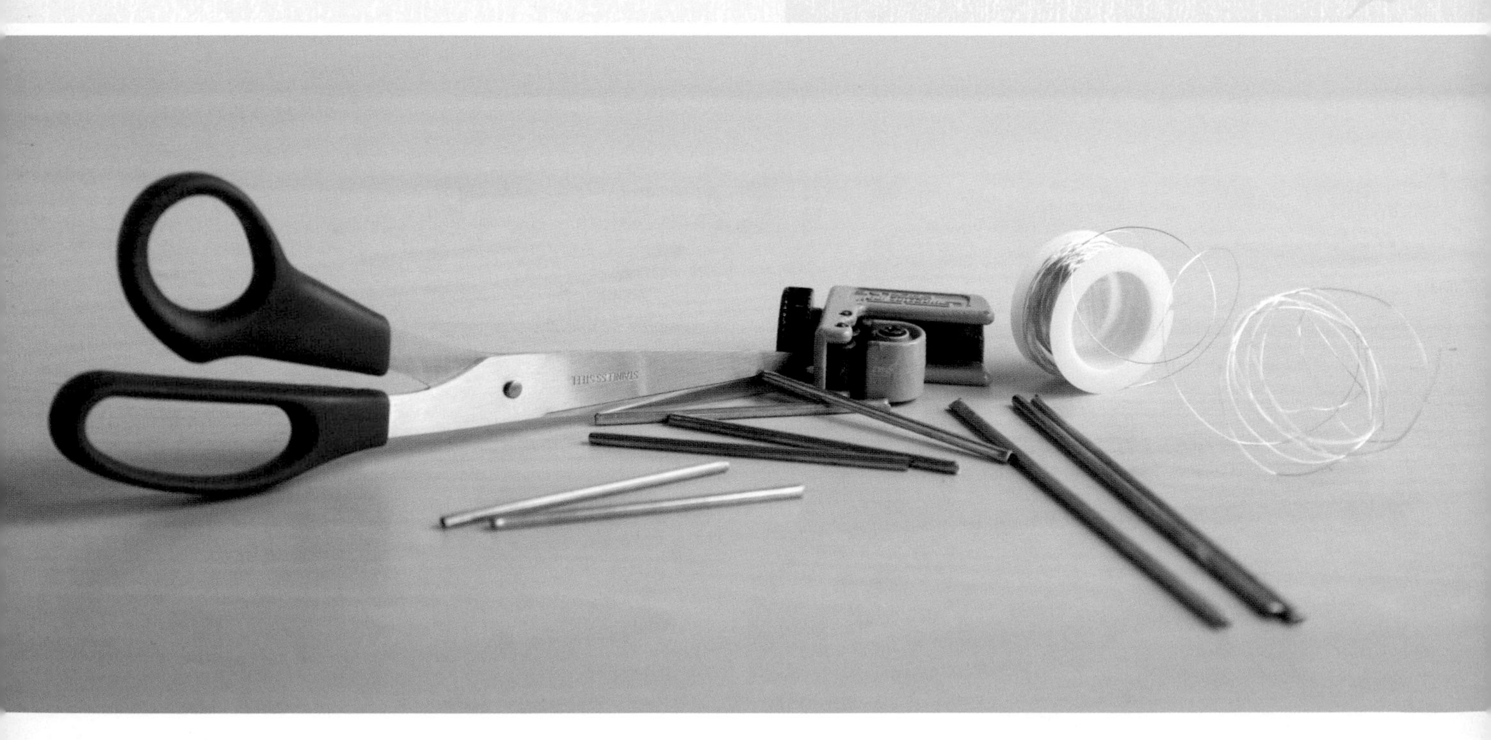

1. **Cut the brass tubing.** To make the small himelli, use the pipe cutter to cut the brass tubing into six 3" (8cm) pieces and three 6" (15cm) pieces.
2. **Begin the planter base.** Leave the brass wire attached to the spool and slide it through 4 pieces of tubing in the following pattern: long, short, short, long. Gently shape these pieces into a diamond shape with the long pieces connecting at the top. Leave a 12" (30.5cm) tail of wire, then twist the wires together. Do not cut the wire from the spool.
3. **Complete the planter base.** String the following pieces on the short wire end: one long piece and one short piece. Attach the wire where the 2 short pieces of your intial diamond shape meet. Knot the wire and cut off the excess. At the top of the planter, trim the wire still attached to the spool to your desired length. Your himelli will hang from this wire; I left mine 24" (61cm) long.

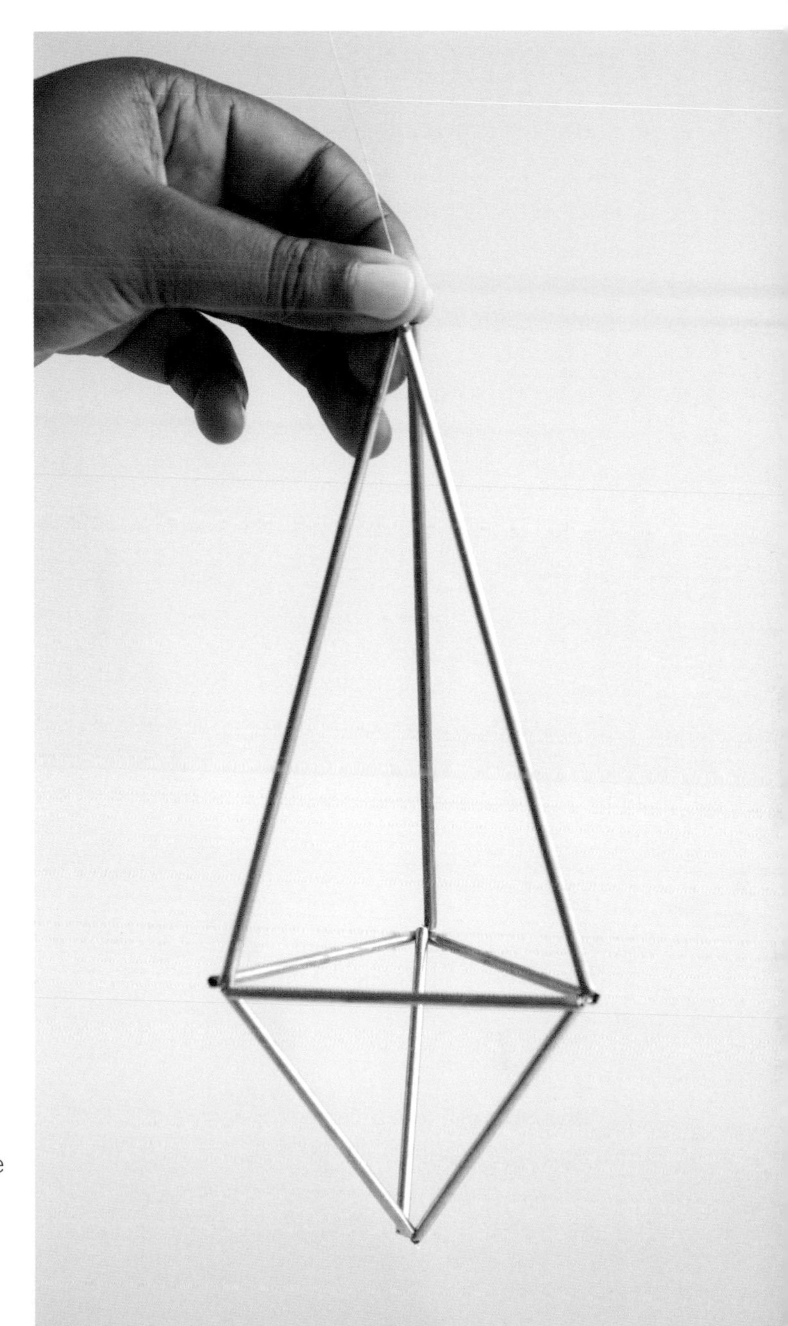

4. **Connect the sides.** Cut a 12" (30.5cm) piece of brass wire. Tie one end of the wire to the point where a long and short piece meet. Thread a short tubing piece onto the wire and pull it across to the next long/short point. Wrap the wire between the long and short piece to secure, then thread another short piece onto the wire. Again, pull it across to the next long/short point and wrap the wire to secure it in place. Repeat this one last time with the final short tubing piece. To finish, tie off the wire and trim the end.
5. **Place the air plant and display.** Place an air plant inside of the planter, gently balancing it in the base, then hang the planter in a place with bright, indirect light. Mist the plant twice a week or as needed.

the star in a jar

COMBINED SUCCULENT TERRARIUM FEATURING THE 'RED STAR' BROMELIAD

bromeliad

4" (10cm) potted *Cryptanthus* 'Red Star'

succulent

2" (5cm) potted *Echeveria derenbergii* 'Painted Lady'

materials

7¼" × 4½" (18cm × 11cm) clear glass carafe

Glass drainage medium* (or white stones)

Activated charcoal

Cactus and succulent soil mix

Air-dried rose Celosia cockscomb

Spanish moss and lichen covered stick**

*The glass medium is a light stonelike material created using 100 percent recycled glass. It provides drainage and doubles as a decorative topper. Any white stones can be used for a similar effect.

**I found this stick out in nature. Look for something similar while you're out on a walk.

1. **Add the glass medium and charcoal.** Pour the glass medium evenly into the carafe, filling it one-fifth full. Add a thin layer of activated charcoal over the glass layer.
2. **Add and slope the soil.** Tilt the carafe slightly backward and add the soil to create a slope. Fill the container one-third of the way full. The slope will help make all the plants visible from the front of the terrarium.
3. **Add the plants.** Unpot all the plants, removing any soil from the roots. With the carafe still tilted, firmly plant the succulent followed by the bromeliad; plant the bromeliad at a 75-degree angle, letting its leaves fan out.
4. **Add supporting items and display.** Place the air-dried rose Celosia cockscomb and the moss- and lichen-covered stick in the terrarium behind the bromeliad and the succulent. Complete the design by covering any visible soil with the glass medium. Place the terrarium in indirect light and water the plants once a week or as needed.

handcrafted mushrooms

CLOSED MINI MOSS TERRARIUM FEATURING CLAY MUSHROOMS

moss

Cushion moss *(Leucobryum)*

materials + tools

4" (10cm) glass syrup dispenser

Sand

Decorative colored glass pieces

Potting soil

Activated charcoal

Wire floral stems

White oven-bake clay

Acrylic paint in various colors

Paintbrush

Scissors

NOTE

Use the decorative mushrooms you make in the simple terrarium shown or add them to any of your terrarium designs for a quirky, woodland vibe. Experiment with color, shape and size.

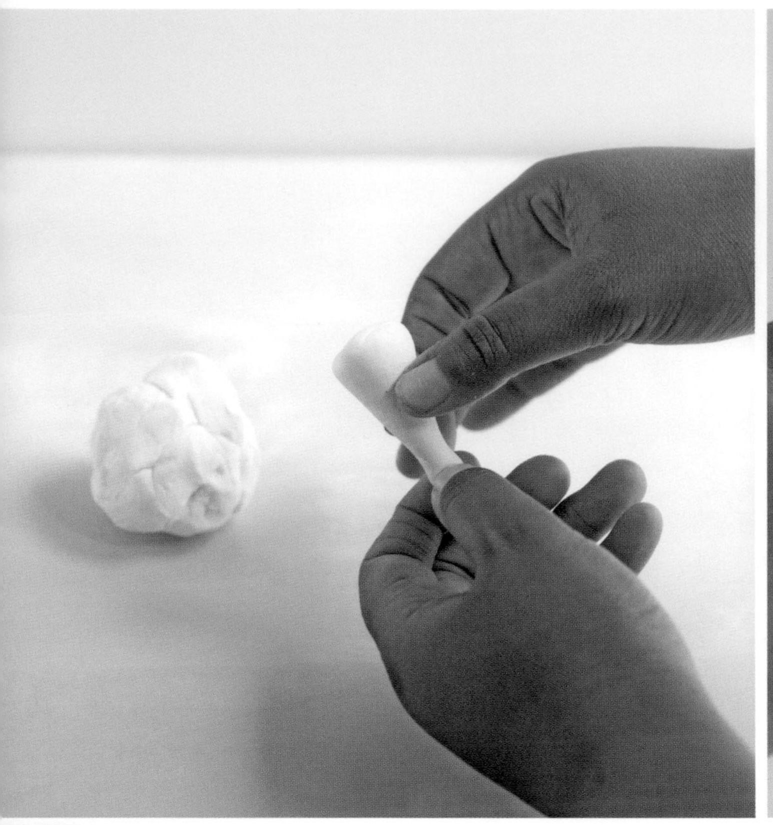

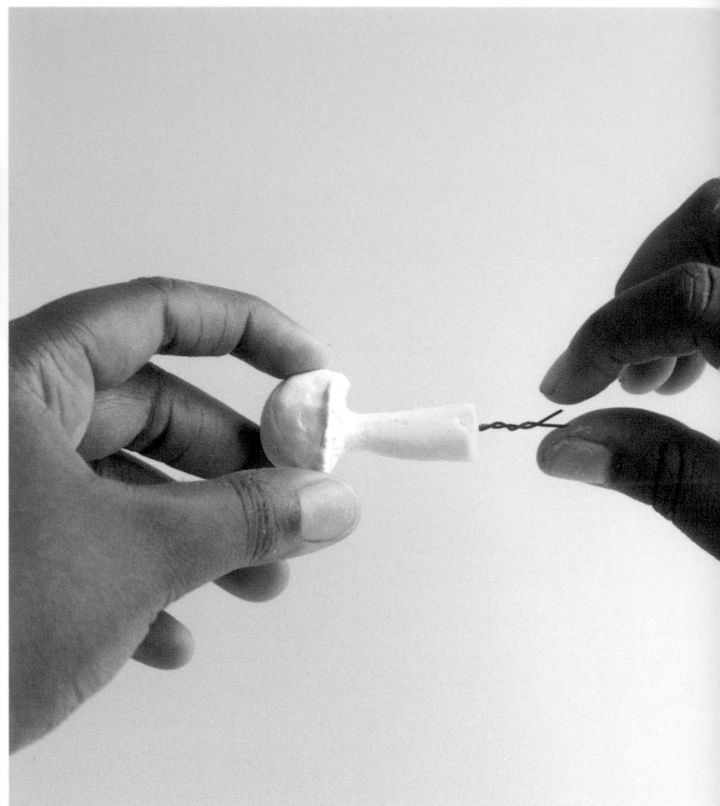

1. **Form a mushroom.** Take a piece of clay and gently roll it with your hands to form a cone shape. Mold the larger end to look like a mushroom cap and the smaller end to look like the stem.
2. **Insert a floral wire stem.** Cut a 5" (13cm) piece of floral wire and bend the wire in half. Gently insert the wire into the stem of the mushroom, twisting it in. Leave 1½" (4cm) of wire sticking out of the stem end of the mushroom. Bake the clay, following the manufacturer's instructions.
3. **Paint the mushroom.** Once it's completely dry, paint the mushroom in your desired colors or pattern based on the colors of the terrarium you'll be using. For the terrarium made here, I chose traditional *Amanita muscaria* 'Fly Agaric' colors and pattern: Paint the mushroom top red, gradually blend in orange and end with solid orange. Let the paint dry completely, then use the end of your paintbrush to stamp white dots onto the mushroom top. Let dry.

4. **Assemble and display the terrarium.** Take the lid off of the syrup dispenser and add a layer of sand to the bottom, filling it one-fifth full. Place a few decorative glass pieces inside the container, then add a thin layer of activated charcoal and soil. Trim your moss to fit in the container and gently place it inside. Stick the wire end of the mushroom into the moss and screw the top back onto the jar. Place your finished terrarium in indirect light. Water your terrarium after assembling, being careful not to wet the clay mushrooms. Because the terrarium is closed, the moss will create a mostly self-sustaining environment, requiring water only 1 to 2 times a month.

mini meditation garden

SUCCULENT TERRARIUM WITH ZEN GARDEN DESIGN

succulents

4" (10cm) potted *Echeveria* 'Lola'

3" (8cm) potted *Sedum morganianum* 'Burro's Tail'

materials + tools

6½" (16.5cm) open-face glass vase

2 small paper bags

5 large decorative river rocks

6 cups fine craft sand

Cactus and succulent soil mix

Knitting needle*

Scissors

*The pointed tip of a knitting needle makes it perfect for drawing in the sand. A wooden dowel can be used, as well.

1. **Cut the paper bags.** Cut off the bottom third of each paper bag.
2. **Plant the succulents.** Open each bag and add the soil mix, filling it two-thirds full. Unpot the plants, removing any soil from the roots. Add a single plant to each bag, making sure that all roots are planted. Gently fold the tops of the bags around the plant so that no soil is visible.
3. **Add plants and sand to the vase.** Gently place the plants in their bags into the vase. Pour craft sand into the vase and around the plants. Cover the bags and soil completely; the bags should not be visible from any angle, to create the illusion that the succulents are planted directly into the sand.
4. **Add the rocks and display.** Rest several large river rocks on top of the sand. Use your knitting needle or wooden dowel to draw a peaceful pattern into the sand. Place the terrarium in bright, indirect light and water the plants once a week (focusing the water on the soil in the paper bags), or as needed.

sandy terrain

SUCCULENT TERRARIUM FEATURING HAWORTHIA + MINERAL ROCKS

succulents

4" (10cm) potted *Haworthia limifolia* 'Fairy Washboard'

3" (8cm) potted *Haworthia fasciata variegata*

4" (10cm) potted *Agave schidigera* 'Durango Delight'

3" (8cm) potted *Haworthia herbacea*

cacti

Two 3" (8cm) potted *Echinocactus texensis*

3" (8cm) potted *Stetsonia coryne* 'Toothpick Cactus'

materials + tools

10" × 4" (25cm × 10cm) glass pan cylinder vase

Cactus and succulent soil mix

Activated charcoal

Sand

Stones

Decorative rocks and pebbles

2 large natural lace rocks*, about 6" (15cm)

2 small pieces of driftwood, no longer than 6" (15cm)

Gardening gloves or newspaper (to protect hands from cacti spines)

*These rocks can be found in the aquarium section of pet stores.

1. **Add the stone and sand layers.** Gently pour the sand evenly into the vase, filling it one-fifth full. Add a layer of stones, filling the remaining space one-quarter full.
2. **Place the mineral rocks.** Position the natural lace rocks inside the vase. Once they're in the desired position, plant them firmly into the stone and sand layers. Continue to hold them while adding the remaining layers to prevent them from falling; your lace rocks should be tall enough to be visible once the plants are added. If they are not, simply plant them on top of the soil layer.
3. **Add charcoal and soil.** Place a thin layer of activated charcoal in the vase, followed by the soil mix, filling the vase another one-fifth.
4. **Arrange and embed the plants.** Unpot all the plants, removing any soil from the roots. Arrange and plant the succulents and cacti starting with the larger plants. Add the smaller plants close to the rocks for a more realistic environment. Take care when planting the cacti; protect your hands from the spines.
5. **Add supporting materials and display.** Add the pieces of driftwood and pour a layer of sand around the plants, covering the soil completely. Finish the design by scattering a few decorative rocks and pebbles across the surface of the landscape. Place the terrarium in bright, indirect light. Water once a week or as needed.

living postcard trio

WIRE PICTURE + AIR PLANT HOLDERS FEATURING AMETHYST ROCKS

air plants

Tillandsia streptophylla

Tillandsia velutina

Spanish moss *(Tillandsia usneoides)*

materials + tools

3 amethyst crystals

3 white, cloth-covered floral stems (26 gauge, 18" [46cm] long)

Preserved reindeer moss

Postcard (or photo)

Pencil

SPECIAL OCCASION IDEA
Replace the postcard with your guests' names for a modern take on placecards at your next dinner party.

1. **Form the foundation.** Take an amethyst crystal and place it on a flat surface to find its natural resting position. Tightly wrap a floral stem once around the crystal, starting and ending on the back side of the crystal. Bend the wire up so it is sticking up vertically from the crystal.
2. **Create a loop for the plants.** Use a pencil as a guide to create a ½" (12mm) circle near the top of the wire.
3. **Add moss.** Place a small patch of preserved reindeer moss into the wire circle and accent it with a small handful of Spanish moss. Make sure the wire can support the reindeer and Spanish mosses without tipping or bending. Widen the circle as needed to better hold the mosses.

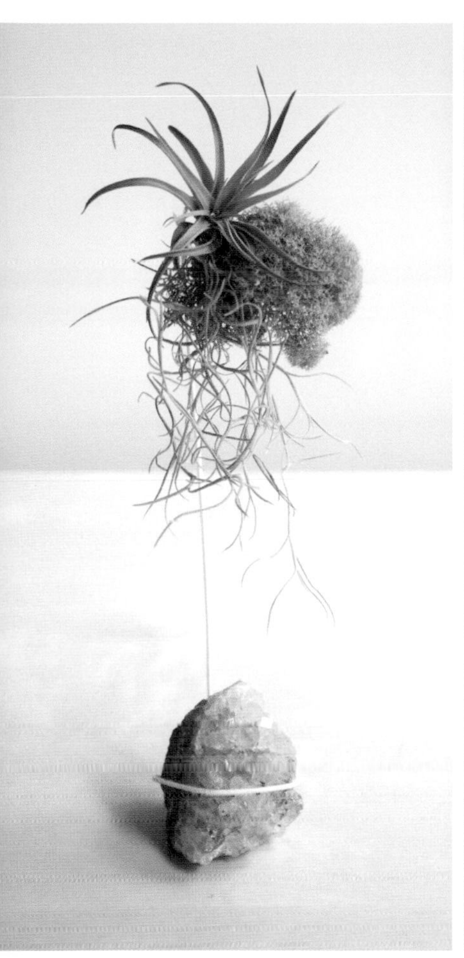

4. **Add an air plant.** Add a single air plant to complete the living plant holder. Again, be careful to balance the plant without tipping or bending the wire. Repeat steps 1–4 to create a second plant holder.
5. **Create a postcard holder.** To create the postcard/photo holder, wrap the wire around the amethyst as you did in step 1. Starting 2" (5cm) from the top of the wire, create a spiral by tightly wrapping the wire around the pencil.
6. **Place a postcard or photo and display.** Place the postcard securely into the spiral (a favorite picture or note can work, too). Arrange your new trio in an area with bright, indirect light and mist the air plants twice a week or as needed, leaving them in their stands.

dino menagerie

SUCCULENT + MOSS TERRARIUM FEATURING CUTOUT DINOSAURS

succulents

6 various 3" (8cm) potted jade plants *(Crassula ovata)* and potted aloe plants

6" (15cm) potted *Ceropegia woodii* 'String of Hearts'

moss

4" (10cm) potted *Selaginella*

materials + tools

6 plastic toy dinosaurs*

Stones

Activated charcoal

Sand

Cactus and succulent soil mix

Spray paint in a variety of colors

Scissors (or a utility knife)

Marker

*Dinosaurs must be hollow.

SPECIAL OCCASION IDEA
These creative planters are the perfect project for a craft party: Make them with friends, then use them as decoration afterward.

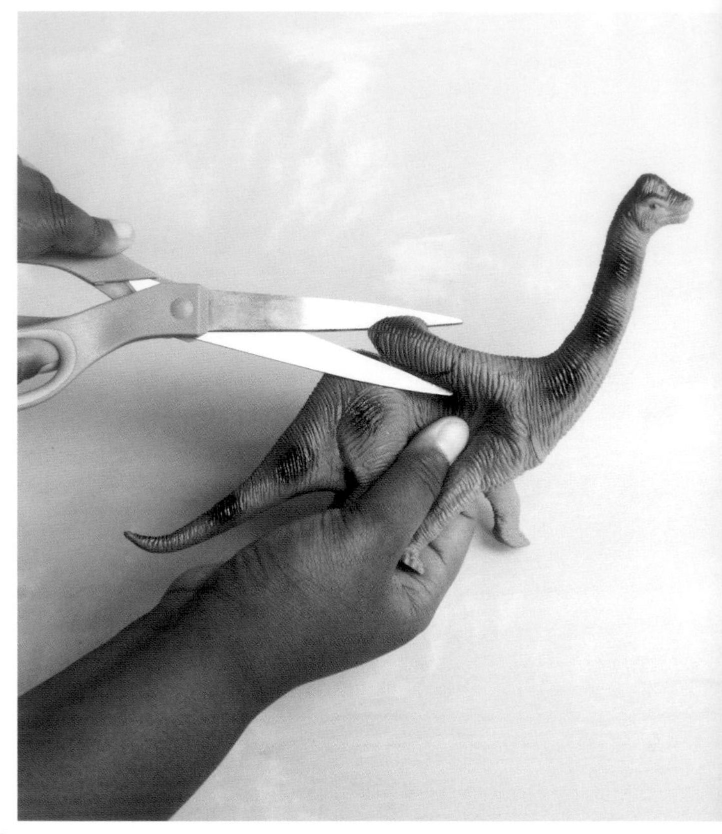

1. **Mark and cut the dinosaurs.** Place one dinosaur in front of you and find the center of the dinosaur's back. Take your marker and draw a 1½" (4cm) circle around the center point. Squeeze the back of the dinosaur, creating a fold in the plastic (this will make it easier to cut), and cut along the marked circle (you can use a utility knife, if needed). Repeat with the remaining dinosaurs.
2. **Paint the dinosaurs.** Following the manufacturer's instructions, spray paint the outside of each of the dinosaurs in the colors of your choice. Let them dry completely.
3. **Build the terrarium layers.** Fill the bottom fifth of the dinosaur with sand. Add a layer of stones, filling the remaining space one-quarter full; cover with a thin layer of activated charcoal. Fill the rest of the dinosaur with soil. Make sure to keep the dinosaur balanced, moving the sand and soil as needed. Repeat the layers in the remaining dinosaurs.

4. **Add the plants and display.** Plant a single aloe or jade plant in each dinosaur and fill in with decorative moss or 'String of Hearts' as you see fit. Place the dinosaurs in indirect light and water once a week or as needed; water the moss more frequently.

the modern bog

TABLETOP MARSHLAND TERRARIUM FEATURING CARNIVOROUS PLANTS

carnivorous plants

4" (10cm) potted *Sarracenia* 'Scarlet Belle'

4" (10cm) potted *Sarracenia leucophylla* 'Tarnok'

4" (10cm) potted sundew plants *(Drosera)*

4" (XXcm) potted *Sarracenia* 'Dana's Delight'

succulent

3" (8cm) potted *Cyanotis somaliensis* 'Furry Kittens' (thrives in consistently moist conditions)

moss

Clump of cushion moss *(Leucobryum)*

materials + tools

14" × 10" (36cm × 25cm) classic glass vase

Brown peat moss

Sphagnum moss

12" (30.5cm) grapewood branch

Plastic bag or bucket (for mixing)

Gloves (optional)

SPECIAL OCCASION IDEA

Use this terrarium as an unexpected addition to the dessert table at your next party. Create a grouping with other tall vases that fit your theme and fill them with plants.

1. **Create the moss mixture.** In a watertight plastic bag or bucket, make a mixture of 60 percent peat moss and 40 percent sphagnum moss. Wet the mosses so they are moist to the touch and mix them thoroughly.
2. **Add the mixture to the container.** Add the moss mixture to the vase, making sure that the bottom is completely filled. Continue to add the mixture unevenly to create a sloped terrain (when the plants are added, this slope will create dimension and a more natural landscape, true to a swamp). Take care to keep the inside of the glass clean.
3. **Add the plants and branch.** Unpot the plants and gently remove some of the soil from their roots; leaving a little soil in the roots will help the plants acclimate to the container. Plant the carnivorous plants first, filling in the back of the vase. Fill in the front with the moss and succulent. Gently add the branch to the container.
4. **Clean the container and display.** Clean the glass if needed and place the terrarium in an area with bright, sunny light. Keep the soil in your terrarium damp to wet at all times; carnivorous plants thrive in consistently wet conditions. Water plants using only purified water or rainwater. Heavily mist the terrarium between waterings in the mornings and evenings to help increase airflow and humidity. If outdoors, carnivorous plants will feed themselves. Indoors, they require feeding 1 to 2 times a month. Place a dried or living insect (such as worms or fruit flies) directly onto the leaves of the plant or inside the pitcher. Weed the terrarium as needed.

wearable landscape necklace

MINI TERRARIUM NECKLACE WITH OMBRÉ-COLORED CORD

materials + tools

1" (30mm) mini glass bottle with cork top

⅗" (15mm) screw eye bails

Neutral-colored suede cord

Fabric dye

Preserved reindeer moss*

Zebra nerite snail shells

Decorative sand

Scissors

Small glass bowl or plastic container (for dyeing the suede)

Latex or rubber gloves (optional)

Tweezers (optional)

*Live sheet moss can be substituted for a living necklace. Pick the greenest pieces and lightly mist before putting the moss in the bottle. Water the moss once or twice a month.

SPECIAL OCCASION IDEA
Make your next birthday party memorable by incorporating this DIY project, perfect for kids of all ages. The necklace is fun to make and a perfect party favor.

1. **Cut the suede cord and prepare the dye.** Cut the suede cord long enough that your necklace will fit comfortably over your head. Prepare your fabric dye bath as instructed on the dye packaging, using a small glass bowl or plastic container to hold the dye.
2. **Create an ombré effect.** Once the fabric dye bath is prepared, hold both ends of the cord and dip three-quarters of the cord into the dye. Hold the cord in the dye for 15 seconds, gently moving the cord up and down to prevent a hard line from forming on the suede. Dip the cord again, this time dipping only half of it into the dye, and hold for 35 seconds, gently moving the cord up and down. Finally, dip one-quarter of the cord into the dye and hold it there, moving it gently up and down, for 1 minute. Let the suede air-dry completely before using.
3. **Connect the bail and create the terrarium.** Take the screw eye bail and twist it into the middle of the cork top. Fill the glass bottle one-fifth full with sand, pouring the sand in at an angle. Place tiny pieces of preserved reindeer moss carefully into the bottle, using tweezers as needed. Add the snail shells, then close the bottle securely with the cork top.
4. **Tie the necklace and wear.** Fold the suede cord in half and thread the loop through the bail. Pull the ends of the cord through the loop and pull to secure. Tie the ends of the cord together at your desired length and you're done. Since there are no living elements inside the terrarium, it requires no extra care.

succulents runneth over

SUCCULENT TERRARIUM FEATURING ACACIA WOODEN BOWL

succulents

Three 3" (8cm) potted *Crassula ovata* 'Gollum'

Two 4" (10cm) potted *Echeveria* 'Perle von Nürnberg'

Four 3" (8cm) potted *Kalanchoe fedtschenkoi* 'Scallops' in various colors

3" (8cm) potted *Sedum morganianum* 'Burro's Tail'

4" (10cm) potted *Kalanchoe orgyalis* 'Copper Spoons'

4" (10cm) potted *Faucaria stomatium*

Two 3" (8cm) potted *Euphorbia trigona* 'African Milk Tree'

materials + tools

10½" × 5" (27cm × 13cm) wooden bowl

Plastic sheet (or bag)

10" (25cm) deep clear plastic plant liner

Cactus and succulent soil mix

Activated charcoal

Sand

Stones

Decorative pebbles

Driftwood pieces (optional)

Wooden dowel

Paintbrush

Scissors

Floral tape (optional)

1. **Protect the wooden bowl with plastic.** Cut the plastic sheet to cover the inside of the wooden bowl and secure it flush to the bowl's inner wall; this protects the wood from moisture. Floral tape can be used to help secure the plastic if necessary. Add the plant liner for further protection.
2. **Add the sand and stones.** Gently pour the sand evenly into the plastic liner, filling it one-fifth full, then add the stones, filling it another one-fifth.
3. **Add the charcoal and soil layers.** Add a thin layer of activated charcoal, then fill the rest of the bowl with the soil mix. Fill to the very top of the plant liner.
4. **Arrange and plant the succulents.** Unpot all plants and remove any soil from the roots. Arrange the plants with the taller ones such as the *Crassula ovata* 'Gollum' and *Euphorbia trigona* 'African Milk Tree' in the center and work your way out. Once you're happy with the arrangement, plant the succulents, starting with the plants at the center.
5. **Clean the arrangement.** Use a paintbrush to dust off soil from the leaves as necessary. Use the wooden dowel to make sure all roots are firmly in the soil.

6. **Add supporting materials and display.** Add more sand to the terrarium to cover the soil. Scatter decorative pebbles throughout the container and add driftwood pieces for added texture, if desired. Place the terrarium in bright, indirect light and water once a week or as needed.

breathing holiday ornaments

GLASS ORNAMENTS FEATURING AIR PLANTS

air plants

Any small, flexible air plants that will fit through the ornament's opening. Try: *Tillandsia ionantha* 'Rubra,' *Tillandsia velutina*, *Tillandsia butzii* and *Tillandsia funkiana*

materials + tools

3 clear glass ornaments*

Preserved reindeer moss in various colors

Embroidery floss or string

6 preserved poppy seed mini pods

Preserved botanicals

Sparkling preserved baby's breath

Lichen-covered stick

Wooden dowel (optional)

*Choose ornaments with holes in their aluminium tops; the plants need ventilation

SPECIAL OCCASION IDEA
These ornaments are perfect for adorning your holiday tree or wreath. Once the holidays are over, stack the ornaments in a decorative bowl, creaing a pyramid. Tuck air plants into any empty spaces to finish this year-round look.

1. **Create the reindeer moss foundation.** Remove the tops from the glass ornaments. Tear off small pieces of the preserved reindeer mosses and carefully place the pieces inside the first ornament, filling one-third of the ornament with moss. Use a wooden dowel to arrange the moss as needed. Repeat with the other ornaments.
2. **Add the mini pods and other supporting materials.** Trim 2 poppy seed mini pod stems to fit into the first ornament. Arrange and place the pods inside the glass. Break off a piece of your lichen-covered stick so it will fit inside the ornament. Carefully place the stick inside the ornament along with small pieces of sparkling baby's breath. Repeat with the other ornaments.
3. **Add an air plant and display.** Carefully add the air plant into the ornament and arrange the contents. Finish by placing the top back on the ornament. Repeat with the remaining ornaments. Hang the ornaments from pieces of embroidery floss in a location with bright, indirect light. Remove the ornament tops and lightly mist the plants twice a week or as needed.

painted airpods

AIR PLANT MINI PLANTERS FEATURING BELL CUPS

air plants

2 *Tillandsia ionantha* 'Rubra'

Tillandsia streptophylla

Tillandsia stricta

materials + tools

Four 3"–4" (8cm–10cm) bleached bell cups (unstemmed)

Craft paint in a bright color

Spray paint in various colors

Painter's tape

Paintbrush

SPECIAL OCCASION IDEA
Try placing these pods on each plate at your next dinner party. They'll add a touch of unexpected greenery and make for a lasting gift for your guests.

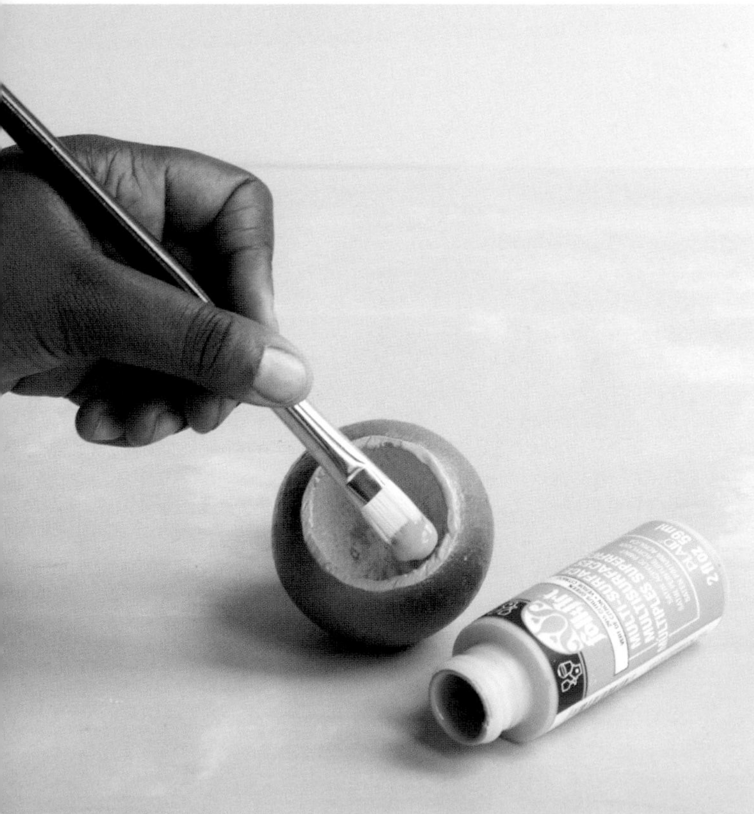

1. **Spray paint the bell cups.** Remove any dirt or debris from the surface of the bell cups with warm water. Let dry completely. Spray paint the exteriors completely, following the manufacturer's instructions on the paint can. Let the cups dry completely (this will take at least 3 hours).
2. **Apply painter's tape and paint the lower half.** Cover the top half of each bell cup in painter's tape. Make sure that all edges are pressed down tightly on the cups so no paint seeps underneath. Spray paint the lower half of the bell cup in a different color, again following the manufacturer's instructions. Let them dry completely.
3. **Paint the bell cup rim.** Use the craft paint and paintbrush to paint the rim of each bell cup. Let this dry completely.

4. **Add the air plants and display.** Place a single air plant inside each cup to complete your planters. Arrange the planters in separate locations or as a group in bright, indirect light. Mist the plants twice a week or as needed.

grapewood greens by candlelight

GRAPEWOOD + SUCCULENT SCULPTURE CENTERPIECE

succulents

Four 4" (10cm) potted *Kalanchoe tomentosa* 'Panda Plant'

Two 3" (8cm) potted *Aloe marlothii* 'Mountain Aloe'

Two 3" (8cm) potted *Haworthia reinwardtii*

5" (13cm) potted *Sempervivum* 'Hens and Chicks'

Two 3" (8cm) potted *Haworthia cymbiformis*

mosses

Two 4" (10cm) potted *Selaginella kraussiana* 'Golden Clubmoss'

Two 4" (10cm) potted *Selaginella erythropus* 'Ruby Red'

Sphagnum moss

materials + tools

24" (61cm) exotic grapewood branch

Three 2"–3" (5cm–8cm) bleached unstemmed bell cups

3 candles

Several 1¼" (3cm) floral greening pins (optional)

E6000 glue

Scissors

SPECIAL OCCASION IDEA
This centerpiece is a great conversation starter at any special occasion. Use it for casual conversation at an outdoor wine party or to create a more romantic vibe with a candlelight dinner for two.

1. **Fill the branch with sphagnum moss.** Find the natural resting point of your branch and pick a focal point. The best focal point is the part of the branch with the most openings, which will allow you to add more plants, anchoring the centerpiece. Fill in most of the openings of the focal point with dampened sphagnum moss; leave some openings empty.

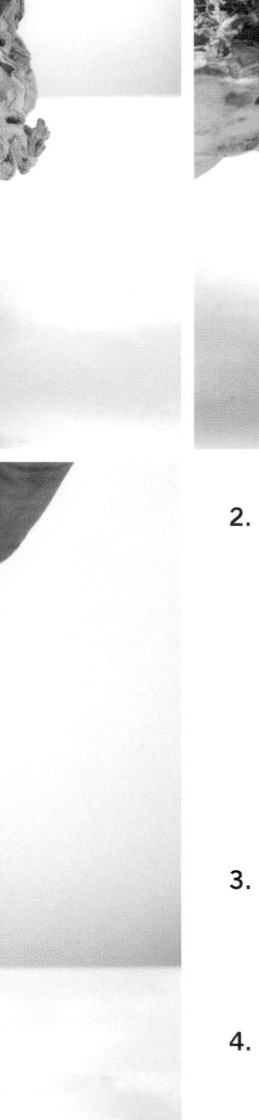

2. **Plant the succulents and mosses throughout the centerpiece.** Unpot all the plants and remove some of the soil from the roots. Arrange the plants before you begin planting. Once you are happy with your design, carefully dig small holes in the sphagnum moss and plant the succulents firmly. Create dense pockets of plants, securely planting the larger ones first and filling in with smaller ones and moss. Use a few floral greening pins to help keep the plants secure, as needed.
3. **Add the bell cups.** Arrange the bell cups on top of the branches, finding relatively flat surfaces on which the cups can rest. Apply E6000 glue to the bottoms of the cups and attach them securely to the branch.
4. **Add the candles.** Once the cups are securely attached to the branch, place the candles in the cups. You may need to adjust the height of each candle so it sticks up just slightly higher than the cup itself.

5. **Clean the arrangement and display.** Use scissors to cut any misplaced roots or sphagnum moss. Display your centerpiece in an area with bright, indirect light. Water once a week or as needed; water *Selaginella* moss more frequently. The centerpiece can be placed outdoors in spring and summer or year-round in warmer climate areas.

desert under glass

CACTUS TERRARIUM FEATURING CONCRETE ACCENTS

succulents

3" (8cm) potted *Haworthia reinwardtii*

cacti

3" (8cm) potted *Espostoa guentheri*

3" (8cm) potted toothpick cactus *(Stetsonia coryne)* or other variety

materials + tools

7" (18cm) glass cloche with rope*

9" (23cm) birch round

Handfuls of sphagnum moss

Cactus and succulent soil mix

Embroidery floss in 3 neon colors

Piece of concrete stone

Gardening gloves or newspaper (to protect hands from cacti spines)

*If necessary, swap out the rope that comes with the cloche for one that better matches the shade of the birch round.

1. **Arrange the container.** Place the birch round onto a flat surface and position the concrete stone on top (this is where the plants will be placed). Make sure the concrete stone fits underneath the glass cloche.
2. **Create nutrient balls.** Dampen a clump of soil and cover it completely with damp sphagnum moss. Make 3 such balls, varying the size of the ball to the size of the plant that will be housed in it. Take colored floss and randomly wrap the floss around the lower half of the ball; leave the upper half bare. Do not cut the floss.
3. **Plant the cacti and finish wrapping.** Carefully unpot the catci, protecting your hands with gloves or newspaper, and remove any dirt from the roots. Create a hole in the top of each ball that is deep enough to reach the soil and place a single plant firmly inside. Continue to wrap the floss randomly around the entire ball, then tie off the floss and cut the end. Do the same with the succulent.

4. **Add the plants and display.** Carefully arrange the plant trio using the nooks and crannies found in the concrete to help secure the plants. You can also rest the plants alongside the concrete if they don't stay put atop the concrete. Cover with the cloche and place the terrarium in an area with bright indirect light. Water once a week or as needed. Because succulents need air circulation to flourish, allow your terrarium to breathe without the cloche for long periods of time; only display inside the cloche temporarily. You can also remove the rope from the top of the cloche to provide better circulation under the glass.

living rim chandelier

AIR PLANT CHANDELIER FEATURING RECLAIMED BICYCLE RIM

air plants

11–14 of the following large, full-sized plants:

Tillandsia bulbosa, Tillandsia filifolia, Tillandsia fuchsii, Tillandsia harrisii, Tillandsia ionantha 'Rubra,' *Tillandsia juncea, Tillandsia magnusiana, Tillandsia streptophylla, Tillandsia tricolor v. melanocrater* hybrid, *Tillandsia velutina,* Spanish moss (*Tillandsia usneoides*)

materials + tools

Six 6" (15cm) hanging glass terrarium vases

Bicycle rim*

Rust-resistant spray paint

Sandpaper (optional)

Two 10' (3m) lengths of ⅜" (10mm) manila rope

Three 3' (0.9m) lengths of black chain

Three ⅝" (16mm) diameter split key rings

Heavyweight fishing line

Ceiling cup hooks (to support and hang chandelier)

Preserved reindeer moss

*I found this bicycle rim at a local vintage market; Etsy.com is another resource to check.

SPECIAL OCCASION IDEA

This living chandelier looks stunning hung from a tree at a rustic backyard gathering or behind the head table at a wedding with a natural vibe.

1. **Spray paint the bicycle rim.** Lightly sand any chipped paint or rust off your bicycle rim before spraying. Once the rim is clean, follow the manufacturer's instructions to spray paint the rim. Let it dry completely.
2. **Mount the hooks and attach the chains.** Choose the location for your chandelier and mount the ceiling cup hooks following the manufacturer's instructions. If you plan on keeping this chandelier up long term, choose a location with bright, indirect light. Take 1 chain and run it through the outer edge of the bicycle rim. Secure the end with a single split key ring one-third of the way up the chain. Take the remaining 2 chains and place them at equal distances from the first chain and repeat the process; you're creating a triangle that will balance the rim while suspended in the air. Hang the rim on the ceiling cup hooks, making adjustments to the chain as needed to balance the rim.

3. **Loop the manila rope and add the terrarium vases.** Take 1 manila rope and tie it securely to the spokes of the bicycle rim. Begin to loop the rope through the spokes, letting the rope hang at various heights. Thread the rope through the top of 1 glass vase and let it hang. Continue threading the rope through the spokes and thread a second vase through the rope. Once the rope reaches its end, tie a single vase to the end of the rope. String the remaining length of rope through the spokes, letting it hang at various lengths. End the second rope by tying on a vase.
4. **Create air plant strings.** Tie the fishing line securely to a spoke; do not cut. Begin to add air plants to the fishing line at various heights by gently wrapping the line multiple times around the base of each air plant. Tle a knot to secure each plant. Continue adding air plants to the line until it reaches your desired length, then cut the fishing line (the longest air plant string

shown is /' [2m]; the shortest is 5' [1.5m]). Add 2 more strings of air plants to the chandelier (3 strings total). To fill in the chandelier a bit more, hang bits of Spanish moss from the rope and fishing line.

5. **Fill the vases and display.** Fill the bottom of each glass vase with reindeer moss and place air plants inside as desired. Mist the plants twice a week or as needed, leaving them in their glass containers.

alphabet garden

HANGING AIR PLANT GARDEN FEATURING WOODEN LETTERS

air plants

11-14 of the following plants per wooden letter:

Tillandsia abdita, Tillandsia bulbosa, Tillandsia butzii, Tillandsia capitata, Tillandsia caput medusae, Tillandsia 'Eric Knobloch,' *Tillandsia fuchsii, Tillandsia funkiana, Tillandsia harrisii, Tillandsia hondurensis, Tillandsia ionantha, Tillandsia juncea, Tillandsia magnusiana, Tillandsia streptophylla, Tillandsia stricta, Tillandsia velutina,* Spanish Moss (*Tillandsia usneoides*)

materials + tools

Three 15" (38cm) unpainted wooden décor letters*

Acrylic paint in various colors

Three 16" × 18" (41cm × 46cm) sheets of preserved adhesive moss (1 sheet per letter)

Preserved mosses

Reindeer moss in various colors

E6000 glue

Sandpaper

Pen or pencil

Scissors

Paintbrush or sponge brush

Hammer and nails (optional; for hanging)

*Look for letters that come with predrilled holes; they make hanging a breeze.

SPECIAL OCCASION IDEA

Change the letters to fit your occasion. I frequently create these for weddings, spelling out "Mr & Mrs" or the couple's initials. You can also hang a single letter from a ribbon and hang it from your front door as an alternative to a wreath during warmer months.

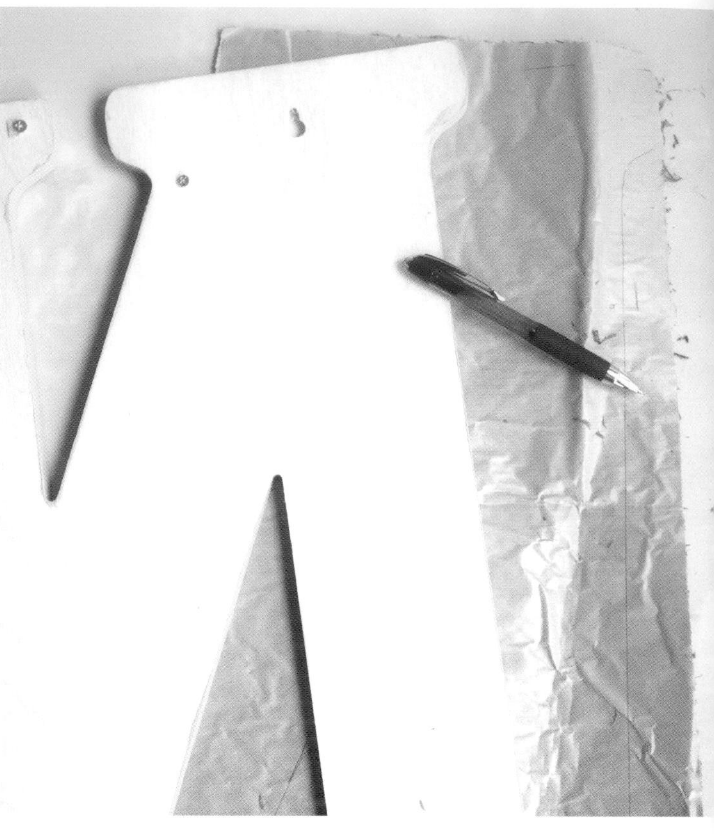

1. **Paint the letter borders.** Lightly sand the surface of the letters to create a smooth surface. Paint the edges of the letters in various colors. Let the paint dry completely.
2. **Trace the letters.** Lay the adhesive moss with the adhesive backing facing up. Place the letters on the moss, flipping them so the mirror image is facing you (don't forget to flip your letters, or the finished letters will be backward!). Trace around each letter with a pen or pencil.
3. **Cut the letters and attach the preserved mosses.** Carefully cut the preserved adhesive moss along the traced lines. Peel the adhesive backing off the moss and stick the moss to the front of the letter. Cut off any excess adhesive moss. Repeat with the remaining letters. Lay the reindeer mosses on top of the letters, arranging them as desired. Glue the mosses in place with E6000 glue.

4. **Attach the air plants and display.** Arrange 11–14 air plants of various sizes on each letter and secure with E6000 glue. Once the glue is completely dry, hang or place each letter in an area with bright, indirect light. To hang, hammer a nail into the wall, leaving one-half of the nail exposed. Hang the letter on the nail from the predrilled hole. Repeat with remaining letters. Mist the air plants twice a week or as needed.

Index

Modern Terrarium Studio. Copyright © 2015 by Megan George. Manufactured in China. All rights reserved. No part of this book may be reproduced in any form or by any electronic or mechanical means including information storage and retrieval systems without permission in writing from the publisher, except by a reviewer who may quote brief passages in a review.
Published by Fons & Porter Books, a division of F+W, a Content + eCommerce Company, 10151 Carver Road, Suite 200, Blue Ash, Ohio 45242. (800) 289-0963. First Edition.

www.fwcommunity.com

19 18 17 16 15 5 4 3 2 1

DISTRIBUTED IN CANADA BY FRASER DIRECT
100 Armstrong Avenue
Georgetown, ON, Canada L7G 5S4
Tel: (905) 877-4411

DISTRIBUTED IN THE U.K. AND EUROPE BY F&W MEDIA INTERNATIONAL
Brunel House, Newton Abbot, Devon, TQ12 4PU, England
Tel. (+44) 1626 323200; Fax: (+44) 1626 323319
Email: enquiries@fwmedia.com

DISTRIBUTED IN AUSTRALIA BY CAPRICORN LINK
P.O. Box 704, S. Windsor NSW, 2756 Australia
Tel: (02) 4560 1600; Fax: (02) 4577 5288
Email: books@capricornlink.com.au

SRN: T4652
ISBN-13: 978-1-4402-4299-1

Edited by Stephanie White; Designed by Clare Finney
Production coordinated by Jennifer Bass; Photography by Michelle Smith

METRIC CONVERSION CHART

To convert	to	multiply by
Inches	Centimeters	2.54
Centimeters	Inches	0.4
Feet	Centimeters	30.5
Centimeters	Feet	0.03
Yards	Meters	0.9
Meters	Yards	1.1
Meters	Yards	1.1

ACKNOWLEDGMENTS

Heartfelt thank-yous to the following people:

Michelle Smith, the book's photographer and all-around Renaissance woman: I am in awe of your creativity, passion and drive as much today as when we first crossed paths. Seeing firsthand how wholeheartedly you have worked toward perfecting your craft has inspired me beyond words. We have worked together, created together and ached together on this project to make it the best: For that, you are a friend for life.

J&C Greenhouses' Jerome and Connie Pittman, for your excitement and unwavering support of my craft and for providing invaluable knowledge. Your stunning succulents make my imagination run wild and heart beat frantically with the urge to design.

Etsy.com for providing me my first global platform to display and sell my terrariums and crafts; it opened the door to countless positive opportunities, including this one.

Amelia Johanson, for recommending and believing in a fresh-faced 24-year-old, only a few steps into the real world; and Stephanie White and the entire F+W team for your dedication and time.

Fairview Greenhouses and Garden Center, KARMOMO Studio's Karm Choi, Richard Rinehart and other fellow artists and businesses used in this book that provided their best works.

My family and friends who have encouraged, loved and helped this dream become reality, especially my brother, M. Harrison George II, and dearest Andrew Cain. Both of you were patient and lent listening ears throughout this process, giving advice both when needed and sometimes unsolicited (both equally appreciated).

My mom and dad, Margaret and Michael George: my foundation, comfort and creative beginning. Thank you both.

MEGAN GEORGE is a social media marketer and terrarium artist. A business school graduate, she combined her education and passion for lush greenery to create The ZEN Succulent, a globally known modern terrarium and crafts small business with customers all over the United States, the United Kingdom, Australia, Switzerland and beyond.

Megan's inspiration lies in her natural surroundings of Raleigh, North Carolina, where she resides, her love for urban gardening and her delight in color. Her terrariums have appeared online on HGTV Gardens and Mental Floss, have been featured on Etsy's Editor Picks and West Elm's Front + Main, and have been published in *The Fayetteville Observer Sunday Life*, and *Our State* magazine.

Active in the East Coast crafting community, she also teaches, writes and leads workshops sharing her modern take on traditional plant terrariums. Visit her at www.theZenSucculent.com and follow her blog at www.theZenSucculent.com/blog.

Find Your Crafty Mojo

These and other fine books are available at your local retailer and online.

31901060619691